From Sudan to South Sudan

African Social Studies Series

VOLUME 41

The titles published in this series are listed at *brill.com/afss*

From Sudan to South Sudan

IGAD and the Role of Regional Mediation in Africa

By

Irit Back

BRILL

LEIDEN | BOSTON

Cover illustration: South Sudanese wait for the arrival of South Sudan's President Salva Kiir at Juba International Airport in Juba on June 22, 2018. Kiir returns from Ethiopia's capital Addis Ababa after a face-to-face meeting with the opposition leader Riek Machar for the first time in almost two years on efforts to end a five-year civil war. AFP Photo / Akuot Chol.

Library of Congress Cataloging-in-Publication Data

Names: Back, Irit, author.
Title: From Sudan to South Sudan : IGAD and the role of regional mediation in Africa / by Irit Back.
Description: Leiden ; Boston : Brill, 2020. | Series: African social studies series 1568-1203 ; volume 41 | Includes bibliographical references and index. | Contents: The emerging role of regional organizations in post-Cold War Africa -- From ecology to mediation : IGAD first efforts as a regional mediator -- We cannot negotiate and fight : IGAD's role in achieving the CPA -- Spring of hope : IGAD's mediation efforts, 2005-2014 -- Winter of despair : IGAD mediation efforts, 2015-2018 -- A comparative view of IGAD's mediation in Sudan, Somalia, South Sudan, and Somaliland.
Identifiers: LCCN 2020022158 (print) | LCCN 2020022159 (ebook) | ISBN 9789004409255 paperback) paperback) | ISBN 9789004425323 (ebook)
Subjects: LCSH: Peace-building--South Sudan. | Peace-building--Sudan. | South Sudan--History--21st century. | Sudan--History--Civil War, 1983-2005--Peace. | Intergovernmental Authority on Development. | Comprehensive Peace Agreement between the Government of the Republic of Sudan and the Sudan People's Liberation Movement, Sudan People's Liberation Army (2005)
Classification: LCC JZ5584.S74 F76 2020 (print) | LCC JZ5584.S74 (ebook) | DDC 341.7/309624--dc23
LC record available at https://lccn.loc.gov/2020022158
LC ebook record available at https://lccn.loc.gov/2020022159

Typeface for the Latin, Greek, and Cyrillic scripts: "Brill". See and download: brill.com/brill-typeface.

ISSN 1568-1203
ISBN 978-90-04-40925-5 (paperback)
ISBN 978-90-04-42532-3 (e-book)

This book is printed on acid-free paper and produced in a sustainable manner.

To Eyal, my beloved husband and steady rock

∵

Contents

Acknowledgments

I would like to thank the Moshe Dayan Center for the Middle Eastern and African Studies, the School of History and the Department of Middle Eastern and African History, all at the Faculty of Humanities at Tel Aviv University, for their financial and academic support in this research. I would like also to thank IGAD's officials at Addis Ababa and researchers from the African Union Peace and Security Programme, Addis Ababa University, for their cooperation, information and support. Special thanks to my editor, Renée Hochman, for her dedication, patience and professional work.

Above all, I would like to thank my beloved family for their intellectual and spiritual support- to my husband Eyal, my daughters and their spouses- Noa and Yogev, Mika and Ariel, Tamara, and the new great addition- my granddaughter Alma.

Acronyms

AGA	African Governance Architecture
APSA	African Peace and Security Architecture
AU	African Union
AUCISS	African Union Commission of Inquiry on South Sudan
AMISOM	African Union Mission in Somalia
AMIS	African Union Mission in Sudan
ARCISS	Agreement on the Resolution of the Crisis in South Sudan
AFDL	Alliance des Forces démocratiques pour la libération du Congo
ARS	Alliance for the Re-Liberation of Somalia
BDF	Botswana Defense Force
COHA	Cessation of Hostility Agreement
CPA	Comprehensive Peace Agreement
CEWRAN	Conflict Early Warning and Response Mechanism
CEWERU	Conflict Early Warning and Response Unit
CODESA	Convention for Democratic South Africa
DOP	Declaration of Principles
DUP	Democratic Unionist Party
EAC	East Africa Community
ECOWAS	Economic community of West African States
ECOMOG	ECOWAS Ceasefire Monitoring Group
GOS	Government of Sudan
GRSS	Government of the Republic of South Sudan
HLRF	High Level Revitalization Forum
HCSS	Hybrid Court for South Sudan
IPF	IGAD Partner Forum
IGASOM	IGAD Peace Support Mission in Somalia
INPFL	Independent National Patriotic Front of Liberia
IGAD	Intergovernmental Authority on Development
IGADD	Inter-governmental Authority on Drought and Development
IDPS	Internally Displaced Persons
ICC	International Criminal Court
ICU	Islamic Courts Union
JMEC	Joint Monitoring and Evaluation Commission
JEM	Justice and Equality Movement
LDF	Lesotho Defense Force
LHWP	Lesotho Highlands Water Project
MVM	Monitoring Verification Mechanism

NDA	National Democratic Alliance
NIF	National Islamic Front
NLC	National Liberation Council
NPLF	National Patriotic Front of Liberia
NEPAD	New Partnership for Africa's Development
AUPSC	Peace and Security Council of the African Union
RECS	Regional Economic Communities
R2P	Responsibility to Protect
RUF	Revolutionary United Front
OPDS	SADC Organ on Politics, Defense, and Security
SNM	Somali National Movement
SANDF	South African National Defense Force
SADC	Southern African Development Community
SADCC	Southern African Development Coordination Conference
SLA	Sudan Liberation Army
SPLA	Sudan People's Liberation Army
SPLM	Sudan People's Liberation Movement
SPLM/A	Sudan People's Liberation Movement/Army
SPLM-IO	Sudan People's Liberation Movement-in-Opposition
SPLM-N	Sudan People's Liberation Movement-North
SAF	Sudanese Armed Force
TFG	Transitional Federal Government (Somalia)
TGONU	Transitional Government of National Unity of the Republic of South Sudan
TNG	Transitional National Government (Somalia)
UNEP	United Nations Environmental Programme
UNMISS	United Nations Mission in South Sudan
UNOSOM	United Nations Operation in Somalia
UNITAF	United Nations Unified Task Force

Introduction

> IGAD…Welcomes the face-to-face talks held on 20th June 2018 between President Salva Kiir Mayardit and Dr. Riek Machar Teny under the auspices of the IGAD Chairperson, H.E. Dr Abiy Ahmed Prime Minister of the Federal Democratic Republic of Ethiopia; … [IGAD] Encourages the two leaders to work together and mobilize the people of South Sudan to end the conflict.[1]

In the almost four decades of mediation efforts by the East African regional organization Intergovernmental Authority on Development (IGAD), its June 2018 Communiqué could be seen as "another brick in the wall," but in contrast to past efforts to mediate between the rivals in Sudan's ongoing civil war, IGAD's present efforts focus mainly on South Sudan, the nation that came into existence as a result of the organization's previous mediation efforts (together with the efforts of many other mediators, to be sure). The fact that such dispute mediation efforts are still very much needed today confirms the importance of IGAD's traditional mediation skills in the turbulent region of the Horn of Africa. At the same time, this new round of conflict resolution efforts also raises many questions about the effectiveness, nature, legitimacy, and other aspects of IGAD's mediation efforts.

This book analyzes the significant shift in IGAD's mediation focus from Sudan to South Sudan. It offers an in-depth exploration of the process itself, including a comparison to other regional mediation efforts, both within IGAD's region and beyond. It also contextualizes IGAD's mediation efforts and their shifting focus from Sudan to South Sudan within the broader context of regional mediation efforts in Africa from the 1990s to the present day. These mediation efforts are analyzed within the evolving theme of African Peace and Security Architecture (APSA), and their achievements and shortcomings are discussed in detail.[2]

In the 1990s, a large number of intrastate conflicts erupted in Somalia, Liberia, Sierra Leone, Rwanda, and other countries in Africa, which were accompanied by a rise in non-combat casualties. These, together with the soaring number of refugees and Internally Displaced Persons (IDPs) in Africa prompted

1 Communiqué of the 32nd Extra-Ordinary Summit of IGAD Assembly of Heads of State and Government on South Sudan, June 21, 2018.

2 Ylönen, "Security Regionalism and Flaws of Externally Forged Peace in Sudan: The IGAD peace Process and its Aftermath," 17.

 DOI:10.1163/9789004425323_002

an understanding that the changing trajectory of violent conflicts there demanded new thinking. Several states responded by attempting to mediate in intrastate conflicts, such Kenya's mediation in Uganda's civil war (1985), Tanzania's mediation in Rwanda's civil war (1992–3), and Tanzania and South Africa's mediation in Burundi's civil war (1996–2003).[3] These efforts, interwoven with discussions on issues related to sovereignty and intervention, eventually led to agreement on the Responsibility to Protect (R2P) principle, which emerged as an important theme in the international discourse of humanitarian intervention at the time.

The spread of violent conflicts in the 1990s, and the multiple humanitarian crises prompted two prominent, influential African thinkers to propose a new approach to issues of sovereignty and humanitarian intervention. The first was Francis Deng of Sudan, who was appointed the UN secretary-general's representative on Internally Displaced Persons in 1993. In a detailed report written with his colleague Roberta Cohen, he stressed the need to reconsider the definition of sovereignty, and proposed to replace it with the concept of "sovereignty as responsibility."[4] UN Secretary-General Kofi Annan from Ghana also called for an expanded understanding of sovereignty. In his article entitled "Two Concepts of Sovereignty," Annan did not challenge the role of sovereignty as the legitimate basis for international order, but proposed that the legitimacy of humanitarian intervention in a sovereign state should be based on the recognition of two concepts of sovereignty: the sovereignty of the state and the sovereignty of individuals.[5]

Such observations by Cohen, Deng, and Annan on the limits that should be set on state sovereignty and the right to intervene in the event of a humanitarian crisis reflected the evolving nature of the discourse on humanitarian intervention and the emergence of R2P doctrine that gradually replaced previous discussions on the limits of "humanitarian intervention." John Siebert, who described the process of defining what R2P actually is can be seen as a "work in progress," explained:

> It is an evolving international norm, yes, but it also rests on a foundation of debate and practice preceding the International Commission on Intervention and State Report. The "Researchers' Preface" to the ICISS background documentation indicates that the R2P concept was founded on previous developments: "The task given to us by ICISS was to lay out in

3 Khadiagala, *Meddlers or Mediators? African Interveners in Civil Conflicts in Eastern Africa*, 1.
4 Cohen and Deng, *Masses in Flights: The Global Crisis of Internal Displacement.*
5 Annan, "Two Concepts of Sovereignty," 49–50.

> straightforward and non-argumentative terms the main issues behind the debate about humanitarian intervention that has taken place over the last decade." The existence of this previous stream of international practice and debate on "humanitarian intervention" did not stop with, nor was it necessarily fully captured or superseded by, the 2001 ICISS report, or by the subsequent official recognition of R2P in the 2005 World Summit Outcome document, paragraphs 138 and 139.[6]

Discussions on the relevance of R2P have become even more relevant today in view of the growth in regional cooperation and regional responses to African conflicts since the beginning of the twenty-first century. Many governments gradually abandoned their commitment to the principle of nonintervention in the internal affairs of independent states, and came to recognize that their shared mutual vulnerabilities require mutual cooperation. This becomes a pan-continental understanding, which marked the transition in 2002 from the Organization of African Unity (OAU) to the African Union (AU) and led to the establishment of peacekeeping forces in Burundi, Sudan, Somalia, and other countries.[7]

The beginning of the twenty-first century also witnessed increasing cooperation between continental and sub-regional organizations in cases that involved conflicts and humanitarian crisis. Khadiagala describes the interesting paradox that emerged with respect to such African cooperation: "While regional institutions are weaker in Africa than elsewhere, the continent's states are continually resorting to them for collective problem solving."[8] This paradox was illustrated by the case of IGAD's intervention in the regional conflicts. On the one hand, IGAD's commitment to values such as R2P is arguably rather insignificant, particularly if tested from a continental perspective:

> When considering Africa's security architecture and the responsibility to protect (R2P), the discussion about the role of sub-regional organizations is usually restricted to Southern African Development Community (SADC) in southern African and Economic Community of Western African States (ECOWAS) in western Africa. The Intergovernmental Authority on Development, or IGAD, whose seven member states (Kenya,

6 Siebert, "R2P and the IGAD Sub-region: IGAD's Contribution to Africa's Emerging R2P-oriented Security Culture," 91.

7 Reno, "The Regionalization of African Security."

8 Khadiagala, "Regional Cooperation on Democratization and Conflict Management in Africa," 3.

> Sudan, Ethiopia, Eritrea, Djibouti, Uganda, and Somalia) comprise the Horn of Africa, is rarely mentioned in this context.[9]

On the other hand, of all Africa's regional organizations, IGAD has accumulated the most experience in prolonged-conflict mediation. IGAD's active mediation between North and South Sudan in the 1990s and the first two decades of the twenty-first century, combined with the unanimous support of the African Union (AU) and other continental and international actors, was translated into the 2005 Comprehensive Peace agreement (CPA) between the south and the north, which eventually resulted in South Sudan's declaration of independence on July 9, 2011.

Unfortunately, the euphoria of the historic achievement of South Sudan's independence was almost immediately eclipsed by the fact that the CPA was not as comprehensive as its title implied: Already in the interim period between the signing of the agreement and South Sudan's independence, numerous gaps and lacunas came to light, sparking many questions regarding the limitations of mediation by local organizations:

> As African regional organizations shoulder more responsibilities for ending conflicts in their neighborhoods, they confront questions about leadership, organizational capacity, and coordination. For weak states trying to mediate civil wars, regional organizations promise the weight of numbers of collective clout, potentially providing the leverage to overcome the inadequacies of unilateral and bilateral initiatives. Yet mediation roles and collective and competitive contexts of regionalism are more difficult to manage, demanding higher levels of coordination.[10]

This observation, which refers to the early period of IGAD's mediation efforts between the north and the south, between 1993 and 1999, was unfortunately relevant again to the internal strife in independent South Sudan, which has escalated since 2013 into a large-scale conflict that demanded the renewal of IGAD's mediation efforts. The fact that many issues that were supposedly addressed in the CPA negotiation phase, including the political, territorial, military, and economic dimensions of power sharing, remained relevant in the negotiations between the rival parties of South Sudan, and that these negotiations

9 Siebert, "R2P and the IGAD Sub-region: IGAD's Contribution to Africa's Emerging R2P-oriented Security Culture," 89.

10 Khadiagala, *Meddlers or Mediators? African Interveners in Civil Conflicts in Eastern Africa*, 187.

ended in the IGAD-led 2015 Agreement on the Resolution of the Crisis in South Sudan (ARCISS) are evidence both of IGAD's persistence, experience, and commitment throughout almost four decades of mediation efforts, and of the weaknesses of these efforts.[11]

Alongside a discussion on the relevance of African peace and security architecture to IGAD's mediation efforts, this book also analyzes the developments of the theme of African Governance Architecture (AGA) in the recent decade. AGA is designed "to foster operational linkages by harmonizing existing governance institutions and mechanisms," and reflects the growing awareness that conflict resolution and good governance are interwoven processes. The AGA also seeks to define "shared Values as a set of core principles for Africa to govern by: basic right to life, participation in governance, equality of persons, justice, adherence to the rule of law, sovereignty, and the interdependence of states."[12] IGAD's commitment to democratization, transition of power, transparency of governmental mechanism and practices that are relevant to the organization's mediation efforts will be discussed in the context of AGA in the relevant book chapters.

The first chapter reviews Western attitudes toward Africa in the post-Cold War era, which tended toward isolationism and non-intervention in internal African conflicts. Although there are several reasons for the development of these attitudes, the consequences of the failed Restore Hope Operation in Somalia in the early 1990s were one of its main catalysts. One of the devastating results of Western abstention from intervention in intrastate conflicts in Africa was the failure to prevent the genocide in Rwanda (1994). In addition, the weak financial condition of the UN and the poor record of its peacekeeping missions demanded renewed thinking by both international and African regional organizations about delineation of roles between international, continental, and regional bodies, and led regional organizations to adopt a more interventionist approach toward intrastate conflicts. During the 1990s and the first decade of the twenty-first century, continental organizations called for improved cooperation with sub-regional organizations, and further development of these organizations' abilities to prevent instability and resolve conflicts. The pioneers among regional organizations to translate the renewed thinking into practice were the Economic Community of West African States (ECOWAS) in

11 For a detailed discussion on the four dimensions model of power-sharing in South Sudan, see: Wight, "South Sudan and the Four Dimensions of Power-Sharing: Political, Territorial, Military, and Economic."

12 Khadiagala, "Regional Cooperation on Democratization and Conflict Management in Africa," 6–7.

Liberia (1990–1997 and 1999–2003), in Sierra Leone (1997–2000), and Guinea-Bissau (1998–1999); and the Southern African Development Community's (SADC) intervention in Lesotho (1998) and the Democratic Republic of Congo (1998).[13] Thus, besides providing the historical and continental background to the case of IGAD's intervention in the Sudanese conflict, the first chapter introduces the analytical framework and conceptual building blocks of the book, mainly with respect to the role of regional organizations in conflict resolution in the 1990s and the two decades of the twenty-first century.[14] The first chapter also outlines a comparative framework between IGAD's region and the other regions of Africa, for example with respect to the lack of a hegemon among IGAD states, in contrast to the regions of ECOWAS and SADC, whose hegemons are readily able and willing to act on or fund collective decisions.

Chapter 2 analyzes IGAD's emerging role as a regional mediator. Its predecessor, the sub-regional organization Inter-Government Authority on Drought and Development (IGADD), was first established in 1986, and its original members were Djibouti, Ethiopia, Kenya, Somalia, Sudan, and Uganda, which were joined by Eritrea after its independence. The states in this region shared common environmental vulnerabilities that create a significantly greater probability of violent conflict, such as large populations of pastoralists (including growing competition for scarce water in pastoralist areas and potential disputes between countries over water), and pervasive poverty.[15]

Indeed, almost since its foundation, IGADD's policies aimed to resolve the interrelated issues of conflicts and environmental hazards. Already in the late 1980s, IGADD's diplomatic initiative was responsible for the historical agreement to re-establish diplomatic relations between the former bitter rivals Ethiopia and Somalia.[16] Yet, it was the ongoing and escalating conflict in Sudan and its regionally destabilizing effects which pushed the organization to assume a more active role in conflict mediation and prevention. This chapter analyzes the organization's transition from IGADD to IGAD in 1996 – from an organization that focused mainly on environmental issues to one whose main focus lies in regional mediation efforts. This chapter, which covers the period from the mid-1980s to the early-1990s, discusses the developments in the Sudanese civil

13 Adebajo, *Building peace in West Africa: Liberia, Sierra Leone, and Guinea-Bissau*; Tavares, "The Participation of SADC and ECOWAS in Military Operations: The Weight of National Interests in Decision-Making."

14 Stein, "From Bipolar to Unipolar Order: System Structure and Conflict Resolution," 6–7.

15 Siebert, "R2P and the IGAD Sub-region: IGAD's Contribution to Africa's Emerging R2P-oriented Security Culture,"94.

16 Adar, "Conflict Resolution in a Turbulent Region: The Case of the Intergovernmental Authority on Development (IGAD) in Sudan," 46–7.

war between the north and the south, and connects them to IGADD's early mediation efforts.

Chapter 3 describes IGAD's initial steps as a regional mediator between the parties representing northern and southern Sudan, which extended from the initial talks in the 1990s to the signing of the Comprehensive Peace Agreement (CPA) in January 2005. This conflict, the longest civil war in post-colonial Africa (1955–1972 and 1982–2005), accounted not only for approximately two million deaths and four million refugees and IDPs, but also spilled over to Sudan's neighboring countries, producing regional instability. This chapter analyzes IGAD's various decision-making mechanisms, which led to the decision to take an active part in the mediation efforts between the rivaling Sudanese parties, and explores the latter's motivation to accept IGAD's role as an active mediator in the process. This chapter offers an in-depth analysis of IGAD's contribution to the CPA's major achievements, including agreement on issues of self-determination, separation of state and religion, and power sharing, yet also examines the main shortcomings of the agreement, such as its lack of comprehensiveness, as a result of which many regions remained outside the agreement, and many groups felt excluded. This analysis is particularly significant, as it offers important lessons to IGAD for its subsequent mediation efforts in South Sudan.[17]

Chapter 3 also analyzes IGAD's use of preventive strategies such as the Conflict Early Warning and Response Mechanism (CEWRAN). This mechanism was initially created by the AU, which recognized the significance of early action to prevent conflict escalation. CEWRAN reflected the belief that gathering information in the early stages of a crisis and analyzing potential responses could contribute to conflict prevention.[18] CEWRAN was designed to cover four main areas: pastoral communities and cattle rustling, small arms and environmental security, peace process, and civil society.[19] Of the continent's regional organizations, IGAD was the first regional organization to operate such a mechanism. The advantages and shortcomings of this mechanism in practice are discussed, including, for example, how disagreements between the members affected CEWARN's activities in cases of cross-border confrontations between pastoralists.

Chapter 4 traces IGAD's involvement in the period following the signing of the CPA until the outbreak of civil war in the newly independent state of

17 Apuuli, "IGAD's Mediation in the Current South Sudan Conflict: Prospects and Challenges."
18 Christensen, "Conflict Early Warning and Response Mechanism in the Horn of Africa: IGAD as a pioneer in Regional Conflict prevention in Africa."
19 Juma, "The Intergovernmental Authority on Development and the East African Community," 239–41.

South Sudan. An analysis of the developments in the interim period leading to South Sudan's independence supports the argument that several major problems that were unaddressed in this period, such as the fate of the "contested regions" (the Blue Nile, Southern Kordofan, and Abyei), led to conflicts in these areas and at the borders between them after independence. Another problematic issue that developed in the interim period is what de Waal termed "the Kleptocratic Club," a leadership that drew its power from the interwoven processes of increasing militarization, underdevelopment, and institutionalization of corruption. As a result, despite generous per capita international funding, most of the budget of South Sudan's transitional government was spent on militarization.[20] In this context, it will be argued that, as a result of its overly lenient attitude toward the governments of Sudan and its lack of a long-term perspective, IGAD did little to prevent the seeds of grave future events from taking root.

The independence of South Sudan in July 2011 was a historic development that challenged post-colonial Africa's sanctity of colonial borders. Notwithstanding its historical achievement, as one of the world's most underdeveloped countries, the nascent South Sudan was an extremely fragile state. Yet, instead of uniting forces to confront the country's enormous challenges, ethno-political interests split South Sudanese society. In mid-December 2013, internal tensions were exacerbated by a power struggle between the President and his deputy. The conflict had a clear ethnic character, as the rivals represent South Sudan's primary ethnic groups: President Salva Kiir represents the Dinka, while his deputy, former Vice President Rick Machar, represents the Nuer. The rivals also had a long personal history, interspersed with various domestic and foreign interests. This chapter describes the background to the development of this conflict, which quickly spread like wildfire and caused one of the severest humanitarian crises of the twenty-first century, compelling IGAD to renew its mediation efforts.[21]

Chapter 5 focuses on IGAD's recent mediation efforts in the civil war in South Sudan, from 2013 until 2018. IGAD responded immediately to the South Sudanese crisis, as is particularly evident from the fact that within four days, its representatives arrived in Juba, along with other representatives from the AU, the UN, and others. Moreover, at the January 2014 peace talks in Addis Ababa, IGAD, the AU, and regional states put pressure to bear on the rivals to sign an agreement on the cessation of hostilities and an agreement on the status of

20 de Waal, "The Price of South Sudan's Independence," 195.

21 "Uprooted by Conflict: South Sudan's Displacement Crisis." Report of the Secretary-General on South Sudan (covering the period from April 14 to August 19, 2015).

detainees. IGAD also sought to extend its authority as mediator by initiating "IGAD-PLUS," a revised process designed to create a unified international front based on the active participation of partners, including the AU, UN, EU, China, United States, Britain, Norway, and others. IGAD wished to use this process to discuss important issues such as the basic power-sharing ratio, transitional governance, and security agreements, and also encouraged the UN to appoint a dedicated political envoy to South Sudan and Sudan. With a role distinct from the peacekeeping mission, the envoy would represent the UN in IGAD-PLUS on issues such as working with member states and with the UN's sanctions committee to ensure the effectiveness of any sanctions imposed on parties that violate the agreements.

Despite its initiative, the inadequacy of IGAD's mediation efforts was revealed once again, for example in its inability to dispel the parties' mutual distrust. Violence and famine continued to increase in severity and spread from the "traditional" conflict areas to new areas that had been peaceful until then. This chapter critically reviews the achievements and setbacks of the current IGAD mediation process, using a comparative approach to the organization's previous role as a mediator between the north and the south.

Chapter 6 contextualizes IGAD's mediation efforts in Sudan and South Sudan within a broader regional perspective and offers a specific comparison to IGAD's mediation efforts in another East African country with a turbulent history. IGAD's involvement in Somalia can be traced to 2005, when the Somalia Transitional Federal Government (TFG) was established in Kenya following two years of IGAD-sponsored peace talks between various Somali clans and factions. In September 2006, the AU endorsed the IGAD Peace Support Mission in Somalia (IGASOM) to support the TFG's relocation to Mogadishu from Nairobi. The invasion of Mogadishu by Ethiopian troops, after the Islamic Court Union (ICU) assumed control there, not only ignited a new wave of internal violence throughout the country, but also illuminated some of the main setbacks of IGAD's mediation. Besides the obvious issue of the military invasion of one IGAD member by another member, IGAD's efforts to mediate in the Somali conflict were also vulnerable to internal discord. Eritrea's suspension of its membership in IGAD was one of several indications of members' declining support for the organization's operations and its struggle to manage the complicated dynamics of regional relationships. One of the issues discussed at length is the multiple memberships of IGAD's member states and their formative effects on the attitudes toward intervention in intrastate conflicts.

A comparison of the cases of South Sudan and Somaliland illuminates the differences between IGAD's positions in these the two cases: IGAD supported South Sudan's separatist aspirations yet was reluctant to support the separatist aspirations of Somaliland. This issue is discussed in the broader context of IGAD's position on sovereignty, intervention, and conflict resolution.

By comparing IGAD's shifting mediation focus from Sudan to South Sudan, and contextualizing this change within the context of the contemporary role of regional African organizations, this book not only illuminates topics such as Peace and Security Architecture, but also integrates a discussion of these issues with reference to the debate on African Governance Architecture, whose relevance for the resolution of many intrastate conflicts in contemporary Africa, including the IGAD region, is becoming increasingly clear to analysts and policy makers.

CHAPTER 1

The Emerging Role of Regional Organizations in Post-Cold War Africa

In 1995, UN Secretary-General Boutros Boutros-Ghali's call for regional security agreements to relieve the UN's heavy peacekeeping burden was particularly relevant to the situation in post-Cold War Africa.[1] There, the hope that the end of the Cold War, which had been characterized by large-scale violent conflicts, would usher in an era of stability and peace, had been shattered almost immediately. Although many internal conflicts that were identified as proxy wars of rival powers in the Cold War were coming to an end, new types of conflicts emerged. The former super-powers were reducing their military support to their former allies in Africa, yet at the same time they were also cutting back political support and economic aid. The resulting political and economic marginalization of Africa caused internal developments that created weakened state institutions, proliferation of small weapons, rise of local powers such as warlords, remnants of national armies, and predatory business organizations (engaged in rough mining, arms dealing, and trafficking in humans and drugs).[2] This environment led to a sharp rise in bitter internal conflicts in states such as Liberia, Sierra Leone, Somalia, and the Democratic Republic of Congo.[3]

Post-Cold War era relations between Africa and the international community were also marked by dual attitudes toward intervention in what were defined as complex emergency situations.[4] Humanitarian intervention had become much more prevalent since the end of the Cold War, and two large-scale international humanitarian missions in the early 1990s (in Somalia and Cambodia) signaled the international community's new commitment to intervene in cases of severe intrastate conflicts. The evolving role of the UN and the

1 Boutros-Ghali, "An Agenda for Peace."

2 Reno, "The Regionalization of African Security."

3 See, for example: Pham, "State Collapse, Insurgency, and Famine in the Horn of Africa: Legitimacy and the Ongoing Somali Crisis."

4 The term "complex political emergencies" became prevalent in the mid-1990s, when it became clear that the new conflict situations in places such as Somalia and Bosnia demanded a broader and more tightly coordinated response. See Duffield, *Global Governance and the New Wars: The Merging of Development and Security,* 12, 14, 52, 65, 71, 86, 89, 95–6, 161–3, 244, 250; 252, 254–5. Smillie and Minear, *The Charity of Nations: Humanitarian Action in Calculating World*, 26–7.

 | DOI:10.1163/9789004425323_003

Security Council, no longer restrained by their former veto-induced paralysis, also resulted in a significant expansion of peacekeeping operations around the world: In contrast to the period from 1948 to 1978, when the UN deployed 13 peacekeeping missions, the UN has initiated 47 peacekeeping operations in more than 15 countries since the end of the Cold War (1989-onward). In addition to increased deployment frequency, UN peacekeeping missions became larger and better equipped, and their mandate clearly defined as the protection of civilians.[5]

This was not, however, the case in Africa, where the traumatic consequences of the failure of Operation Restore Hope in Somalia in 1993 and the absence of international intervention in the genocide in Rwanda in 1994 (both discussed later) resulted in a more general abstention from international intervention. According to Ylönen, "In the context of Afro-pessimism following the Rwandan genocide and the failed external intervention in Somalia, Western states had by the mid-1990s become increasingly inclined to reduce spending on international peacekeeping missions in Africa."[6] Thus, many conflict resolution, mediation, peace-building and peacekeeping tasks in the 1990s were left to the African states, which developed a common understanding of their shared vulnerabilities, and awareness of the need to combine forces to tackle challenges such as "disarming and demobilizing warring factions; conducting and observing elections; repatriating and resettling refugees; rehabilitating and reintegrating soldiers into local communities; reconstructing and reforming security forces, civil services, and judiciaries; monitoring and investigating human rights abuses; and overseeing transitional civilian authorities."[7]

The idea of "African solutions to African problems" was often coupled with the slogan "African 'sub-regional' solutions to African 'sub-regional' problems."[8] Consequently, regional organizations' involvement in local African interstate, but mostly intrastate, conflicts gradually expanded, such as the mediation efforts launched by the regional organization IGAD between the rival parties of Sudan. To provide both the background and a comparative perspective for the case of IGAD, this chapter focuses on the efforts of the regional organizations ECOWAS and SADC to "make a difference" through conflict resolution

5 Weiss, *Humanitarian Intervention: Ideas in Action*, 38–9.

6 Ylönen, "Security Regionalism and Flaws of Externally Forged Peace in Sudan: The IGAD Peace Process and its Aftermath,"16–17.

7 Adebajo, *Building peace in West Africa: Liberia, Sierra Leone, and Guinea-Bissau*, 19.

8 Adar, "Conflict Resolution in a Turbulent Region: The Case of the Intergovernmental Authority on Development (IGAD) in Sudan," 43.

and mediation in the western and southern regions of the continent.[9] After a brief background on the establishment of ECOWAS and SADC, the chapter proceeds to review their peacekeeping efforts during the 1990s, and concludes by analyzing the advantages and limitations of the regional mediation efforts that were integrated in endeavors to create a continental peace and security architecture.[10]

The roots of the involvement of the Economic Community of West African States (ECOWAS) in Liberia, Sierra Leone, and Guinea-Bissau can be traced to the post-colonial context of independent states struggling to define their regional status. Yet, as this chapter focuses mainly on the 1990s, mention of only two essential observations of the period from independence to the 1990s is warranted here. First, West Africa can be defined as a region with a hegemon. Nigeria's discovery of oil during the 1960s, combined with its strategic location and the fact that Nigeria is a demographic giant (the most populated country in Africa), defined its status as a local "Gulliver" or hegemon.[11] Second, the heritages of different colonial regimes continued to define interstate relations, informing alliances and rivalries in the region in the decades after independence, and impeding many attempts to foster regional integration, whether in the economic, political, or security fields. The true depth of the chasm between former French and British colonies, and more particularly between Nigeria and the dominant Francophone states of West Africa, such as Senegal and Côte d'Ivoire, was revealed when efforts focused on establishing a major regional organization.[12]

ECOWAS was established in 1975, following almost two years of negotiations. Fifteen West Africa states signed the Treaty of Lagos in May that year, and were quickly followed by Cape Verde, which joined as the sixteenth member. As was the case with most African regional organizations, the initial goals of the fledgling organization were almost entirely unrelated to security and focused on issues such as elimination of custom duties and trade restrictions. This focus, as well as member states' lack of political and economic commitment, may explain why ECOWAS appeared to be an ineffective tool for regional integration in the first 15 years of its existence. Many states also were intimidated by Nigeria's hegemonic role in ECOWAS, and preferred to

9 Aning, "The Challenge of Civil Wars to Multilateral Interventions"; Levitt, "Conflict Prevention, Management, and Resolution: Africa – Regional Strategies for the Prevention of Displacement and Protection of Displaced Persons: The Cases of the OAU, ECOWAS, SADC, and IGAD."

10 Vines. "A Decade of African Peace and Security Architecture."

11 Adebajo, *Building Peace in West Africa: Liberia, Sierra Leone, and Guinea-Bissau,* 23–42.

12 Bach, "The Politics of West African Economic Co-Operation: C.E.A.O. and E.C.O.W.A.S.".

operate through rival organizations such as the Francophone Communauté Économique de l'Afrique de l'Ouest (CEAO).[13] In the early 1990s, as conflicts in the region escalated and increasingly threatened regional stability, ECOWAS gradually shifted its attention to security issues, as did most regional organizations in Africa.[14] The theoretical dimension of this shift and its practical aspects are discussed in Chapter 2.

The target of ECOWAS's first significant intervention involving conflict resolution, mediation, peace-building, and peace keeping was the civil war in Liberia, between 1989 and 1997 (and subsequently, between 1999 and 2003). Initially, Samuel Doe's *coup d'état* in April 1980 was viewed as a genuine national revolution marking the end of 144 years of Americo-Liberian hegemony and the transfer of power to the indigenous people of Liberia, but it soon became clear that the old oligarchy had been replaced by an ethnic junta that had no intention of establishing a democratic republic with equal representation for Liberia's sixteen ethnic groups, and was not averse to using violent and oppressive measures to reinforce its control. Shortly afterward, opposition groups comprising the National Patriotic Front of Liberia (NPLF) led by Charles Taylor, and Prince Johnson's Independent National Patriotic Front of Liberia (INPFL) began to challenge the new regime's oppressive and dictatorial practices. The three military forces eventually turned on each other, leading to the total destruction of Liberia. As warlords assumed control of different parts of the country, ethnic slaughter reached a massive scale and created a huge refugee problem, which spilled over to Liberia's neighboring countries and threatened regional stability.[15]

The civil war, which claimed an estimated 200,000 lives,[16] and the grave internal and external implications of the collapse of the Liberian state, prompted ECOWAS leaders to look for peacekeeping and peace enforcement solutions. In May 1990, ECOWAS heads of state met in Banjul, Gambia, and established the ECOWAS Ceasefire Monitoring Group (ECOMOG). ECOMOG's mission in Liberia was to achieve an immediate cease-fire, establish an interim administration in Monrovia, and set in motion a process of nationwide elections that

13 *Ibid.*

14 Brown, "Why Regional Economic Organizations Take on Conventional Security Tasks?".

15 For a detailed description of the causes of the breakout of the Liberian civil war, its main developments, and regional and international attempts to solve the conflict, see Aboagye and Bah, *Tortuous Road to Peace: The Dynamics of Regional, UN and International Humanitarian Interventions in Liberia*; Adekele, "The Politics and Diplomacy of Peacekeeping in West Africa: The ECOWAS Operation in Liberia."

16 On the estimated toll of loss of lives, see: Final Report of the Secretary-General on the UN Observer Mission in Liberia, S/1997/712/12, September 1997, 5.

ECOMOG would also monitor.[17] In July 1990, a blueprint for an ECOWAS military intervention was announced, and the first ECOMOG force landed in Monrovia the following month. Yet, it soon became clear that the new force was unable to control the situation on the ground, primarily due to its failure to secure the cooperation of some of the local forces. The NPLF, for example, opposed the intervention, claiming that ECOMOG prevented Prince Johnson from translating his military victory into political representation by attempting to force him to make peace.[18]

The internal disputes and acrimony within ECOWAS, such as the conflicting views of Côte d'Ivoire and Burkina Faso on the legitimacy of intervention in internal conflicts, were another important source of the mission's ineffectiveness in its initial deployment stage. Moreover, while some states supported NPLF, others supported various anti-NPLF factions. The result was the continuation of the civil conflict and its devastating consequences.[19] The polarized debate over the intervention's legality and procedures would be repeated in subsequent cases of intervention in intrastate conflicts and would ultimately undermine ECOWAS's efforts to protect civilians.

The ECOWAS mission was the first large-scale attempt of a regional West African organization to intervene in a case that could be defined as a "complex political emergency," one that required a system-wide response by the international community that might include coordination and collaboration between UN agencies, donor governments, NGOs, and military establishments. In fact, a framework for cooperation between the UN and ECOWAS was established following UN Security Council Resolution 866, adopted in September 1993.[20] This resolution was considered unprecedented, as it determined a joint framework of cooperation, and more broadly, it created a foundation for coordination between international and regional organizations regarding intervention in domestic conflicts in Africa.[21] A different sort of collaboration between regional and international organizations in the case of IGAD's intervention in Sudan and South Sudan is discussed in Chapters 3 and 4.

The ECOWAS intervention in the civil war in Sierra Leone, which lasted from 1991 to 2002, sheds light on another factor that contributed to the outbreak of

17 Adekele, "The Politics and Diplomacy of Peacekeeping in West Africa: The ECOWAS Operation in Liberia."

18 Adebajo, *Building Peace in West Africa: Liberia, Sierra Leone, and Guinea-Bissau.*

19 Aboagye and Bah, *Tortuous Road to Peace: The Dynamics of Regional, UN and International Humanitarian Interventions in Liberia.*

20 United Nations Security Council, "Report of the Secretary-General on Liberia," Security Council Documents s/26422, 4.

21 Adibe, "The Liberian Conflict and the ECOWAS-UN Partnership."

interstate conflicts and their effect on regional instability: the poor economic condition of many African states and the economic inequality between them. The colonial partition of Africa was responsible for creating resource-rich countries alongside countries that were almost completely devoid of natural resources. While the existence of natural resources is arguably not necessarily an indicator of citizens' wealth and welfare, the regional organization of West Africa contained some of the poorest countries in the world, such as Sierra Leone, Benin, Gambia, and Upper Volta (which became Burkina Faso). In many cases, these countries' economic weakness was translated into a sense of political inferiority within the regional organization and concerns that the poor states would be swallowed by the richer ones.

A case in point was post-colonial Sierra Leone, which experienced political instability, poor economic development, and insufficient external aid, even compared to other African states. By 1991, Sierra Leone had dropped to lowest position on the UN Human Development Index. That year, a group named the Revolutionary United Front (RUF), led by former army corporal Foday Sankoh, instigated massive attacks against civilians. As in other rebel movements, the rebels' ideological motives were soon diverted from democratic change and justice to attempts to seize control of the country's economic resources, and especially its rich diamond fields. By 1995, country-wide destruction reached overwhelming proportions, with thousands dead, and hundreds of thousands of refugees and Internally Displaced Persons (IDPs). The devastation not only crushed the economy, which racked up an external debt equal to 177% of the GNP, but also caused the total destruction of infrastructures, including 70% of the country's schools and almost total elimination of healthcare centers. RUF committed horrific acts of violence against civilians, including the widespread use of sex slaves, child soldiers, and especially mass amputations of civilians, which came to be known as the symbol of that war.[22] The situation in Sierra Leone could be categorized under the emerging category of conflicts known as the "new wars." This term typically refers to the post-Cold War wars since the 1990s, especially in Africa, characterized by changing relations between the sovereign state and the multiple internal and external actors and stakeholders, all struggling to define their position within the state, creating a situation that is also defined as "durable disorder."[23]

From a regional perspective, the civil war in Sierra Leone plainly illustrated the dangers of a spillover effect. From the outset it was evident that the conflict in Sierra Leone was interwoven with the conflict in Liberia. Close ties between

22 Gberie, *A Dirty War in West Africa: The RUF and the Destruction of Sierra Leone*, 14–15.

23 Duffield, *Global Governance and the New Wars*, 164–5.

Charles Taylor and the Sankoh-led RUF, which were cemented through their involvement in diamonds and arms trade, fueled the Sierra Leone war to create what was described as a "post-Cold War proxy war."[24]

The international community was clearly unable to address the growing refugee and IDP population, control widespread hunger and disease, or stop unchecked violence in Sierra Leone. Although an Inter-Agency Mission to West Africa, led by UN Assistant Secretary-General Ibrahima Fall, advised the UN Security Council to adopt a clear approach in regard to the region's interconnected conflicts,[25] the UN Security Council failed to pass effective resolutions concerning Sierra Leone, and only partially carried through on its financial promises. United States mediation efforts led to the dubious Lomé Agreement of 1999, which forced Sierra Leone President Tejan Kabbah to include RUF fighters as potential members of the government, award an "absolute and free pardon and reprieve to all," and grant the vice-presidency to RUF commander Foday Sankoh. The international failure to resolve the conflict, combined with the conflict's potential spill-over effects, motivated regional actors to come to grips with the situation using their own means.[26]

When over 500,000 refugees from Sierra Leone fled to neighboring Guinea and Liberia as a result of this civil war, ECOWAS felt compelled to provide solutions to resolve the conflict in Sierra Leone. Naturally, the desire to relieve the situation also called into question the identity of the legitimate partners for the dialogue process: What other civil society elements should be included? Could an agreement be reached even if some of the main actors, such as former warlords, were excluded from the mediation process and power-sharing agreements?

ECOWAS's involvement in the protracted Sierra Leone civil war can be divided into three phases. The first phase, from 1991 to 1997, involved Nigerian, Ghanaian, and Guinean troops that provided support and security to various local regimes against the RUF, and included the establishment of an elected government and signing of the Abidjan peace agreement in 1996. The second phase, from 1997 to 1999, was characterized by significant ECOMOG involvement in Sierra Leone in response to an army coup in 1997. Actions included the establishment of ECOMOG II in 1999, and the announcement of the ECOWAS Peace Plan for Sierra Leone the following year in Conakry, but the organization's efforts to stabilize the situation in Sierra Leone in this phase were significantly

24 Francis, *Uniting Africa: Building Regional Peace and Security Systems*, 160.

25 *Ibid.*, 18.

26 Smillie and Minear, *The Charity of Nations: Humanitarian Action in a Calculating World*, 31–3.

hampered by the complex relations among ECOWAS members, including criticism against Nigerian dominance in ECOWAS, which dictated the country's prominent role in the diplomatic efforts to settle the conflict, and its contribution to ECOMOG troops and financial aid. Nigerian officials, on their part, complained that Nigeria was carrying most of the financial and military burden, and Nigerian President Olusegun Obasanjo claimed as much in his address to the UN General assembly in 1999: "Nigeria's continual burden in Sierra Leone is unacceptably draining Nigeria financially. For our economy to take off, this bleeding has to stop."[27] The third phase continued from 1999 to 2001 and included the withdrawal of Nigerian soldiers from Sierra Leone soil, the establishment in 1999 of the more internationally diverse force of (UNAMSIL), United Nations Mission in Sierra Leone which, combined with British military intervention, ended the harsh decade-long civil war.[28]

In contrast to Nigeria, which was recognized (notwithstanding the criticism against it) as a legitimate intervener in western Africa, South Africa was considered an illegitimate hegemon in southern Africa until the end of the white-minority rule in 1991, and some distrust of its motives persisted into the post-apartheid era. Comparing the capacities of the two hegemons during the 1990s, Adebajo and Landsberg claimed:

> The apartheid-era army's destabilization of its neighbors has left a profound distrust of South African military interventionism, which remains strong today. During the 1990s, Nigeria was willing but unable to carry out swift and decisive military interventions in West Africa. South Africa was more able but largely unwilling to undertake such military actions in southern Africa. South Africa has military and economic capacity but lacks the legitimacy to play a hegemonic role. Nigeria arguably has more legitimacy in its own subregion but lacks the military and economic capacity to act as an effective hegemon.[29]

Although Nigeria's efforts to entrench its position as regional hegemon were challenged by France and its Francophone allies in West Africa, and it was accused of being an undemocratic state that ironically aimed to impose democratic regimes on its neighbor states, the accusations against pre-1991 South

27 Quoted in Adebajo, *Building peace in West Africa: Liberia, Sierra Leone, and Guinea-Bissau*, 90.

28 For a detailed discussion on the developments in the different phases, see: *ibid.*, 79–110. For the case of ECOWAS intervention in Guinea-Bissau see *ibid.*, 111–36.

29 Adedajo and Landsberg, "South Africa and Nigeria as Regional Hegemons," 172.

Africa were much graver. Besides its apartheid white-minority rule, South Africa had an "apartheid nuclear bomb" and a flourishing arms industry. These facts, combined with its significant economic power, fueled the view of South Africa as a source of regional destabilization and illegitimate regional power. In fact, the first regional organization in southern Africa, the Southern African Development Coordination Conference (SADCC), was established in 1980 to promote regional integration and reduce dependence on apartheid-ruled South Africa. Only in January 1992, more than a decade later, following the treaty of Windhoek, did post-apartheid South Africa join the organization, which became known as SADC.[30]

As was the case with other regional organizations of the period, SADC's initial objectives focused on promoting regional integration rather than on security tasks. The organization was plagued by many obstacles and problems in its early years, caused by institutional weakness or general crisis such as the HIV/AIDS pandemic, which was particularly prevalent in southern Africa.[31] In the second half of the 1990s, however, SADC's image as an ineffective organization changed as it became more intensely involved in regional issues, particularly following the establishment of SADC Organ on Politics, Defense, and Security (OPDS) in 1996. The new mechanism's activities were directed toward security tasks, including intervention in interstate and intrastate conflicts, with the broad aim of consolidating coherent regional security architecture. Moreover, its institutional framework granted the OPDS relative decision-making and operating autonomy:

> The SADC Organ of Politics, Defense and Security shall operate at the Summit level and shall function independently of other SADC structures. The Organ shall also operate in a Ministerial and technical levels. The Chairmanship of the Organ shall rotate on an annual and on a troika basis.[32]

Although the founding protocol also called for the establishment of a second organ to address interstate security issues, many disagreements and disputes revolved around the interpretation of the Protocol, particularly regarding

30 Baregu and Landsberg, "Introduction" in *From Cape to Congo*, 2–3.

31 See, for example: *SADC Regional Human Development Report 2000: Challenges and Opportunities for Regional Integration*, 147–59.

32 SADC, "Protocol on Politics, Defense and Security in Southern Africa Development Community (SADC) region," 1. See also: *SADC Regional Human Development Report 2000: Challenges and Opportunities for Regional Integration*.

intervention in intrastate affairs.[33] The arguments did not remain solely at the theoretical level, as soon after the SADC adopted resolutions that defined the common features of intervention, the organization became an active regional intervener. Even as Nigeria led ECOWAS in its missions in Sierra Leone, Liberia, and Guinea-Bissau, South Africa led SADC's interventions in Burundi, Lesotho, and the DRC. It is important to briefly review these three missions, as many of their features correspond to IGAD's intervention in Sudan and South Sudan, and are more broadly relevant to issues of regional intervention and mediation in intrastate conflicts.

The conflict in Burundi erupted after President Melchior Ndadaye's assassination in 1993, and escalated after Ndadaye's successor was killed in 1994 in a tragic plane crash together with the president of Rwanda. The violent power struggle in Burundi between the Hutu and the Tutsi gradually deteriorated into open comprehensive civil war in 1995, persisting until 2005, with varying degrees of violence.[34] The conflict in Burundi was directly connected to the civil conflict in neighboring Rwanda, where competition for political dominance between the Hutu and the Tutsi ethnic groups led to the well-known genocide of 1994. As international and continental attention focused mainly on the devastating effects of the Rwandan genocide, events in Burundi were relatively marginalized for almost two years, and only in March 1996 did the OAU appoint former Tanzanian President Julius Nyerere as mediator between Burundi's rival groups. In view of Nyerere's failure to find a common ground for negotiations, a regional summit was convened, attended by the presidents of Tanzania, Rwanda, Uganda, Kenya, and Ethiopia, who suggested a variety of solutions to the conflict, such as economic sanctions, inclusion of various Rwandan interest groups in the power-sharing process, and cooperation with international and regional organizations.[35]

Little progress to resolve the dispute occurred, however, before Nelson Mandela actively entered the mediation arena in January 2000, an act that marked the watershed moment in the mediation process in Burundi for several reasons. First, Mandela's well-recognized prestige as the ultimate African freedom fighter significantly facilitated his efforts to bring the parties involved in the conflict together and kick-start the negotiations between them. The personal factor – the mediator's prestige, charisma, and/or abilities – which is known to

33 Baregu, "Economic and Military Security,"22–3.

34 For a detailed description of the Burundi civil war and the regional mediation efforts in it, see: Bentley and Southall, *An African Peace Process: Mandela, South Africa and Burundi*; Miti, "South Africa and Conflict Resolution in Africa: From Mandela to Zuma." See also Shillinger, *Africa's Peace Maker? Lessons from South African Conflict Mediation.*

35 Miti, *ibid.*, 28.

play a crucial role in mediation processes, is discussed further, for example, in the context of the Kenyan President Daniel Arap Moi's mediation efforts of IGAD in Sudan.

Second, inspired by the Convention for Democratic South Africa (CODESA) process, which was seen as a model for conflict resolution on the continent, Mandela promoted several relatively effective steps directed at conflict resolution, such as the split of a three-year transition period into two equal 18-month periods, in order to create a more gradual introduction of the power-sharing process. Indeed, on July 23, 2001, the Arusha Accord, which was in many respects Mandela's personal achievement as a mediator, was signed, and the date for the formation of the transitional government was scheduled for November that year. The achievements were, nonetheless, accompanied by many setbacks including the exclusion from the agreement of major armed groups, and the signing of the peace accord without a cease fire, ultimately resulting in the continuation of the civil war until 2005, and in many respects, the continuation of hostilities to the present.[36] These setbacks were also lessons that should have been learnt by subsequent mediation efforts and peace building efforts, as discussed below.

In comparison to the case of regional intervention in Burundi, the decision to intervene in the internal affairs of the kingdom of Lesotho, a small landlocked country completely surrounded by South Africa, was not triggered by the eruption of a violent civil war, but by the unstable political environment following the 1998 elections and the resulting dissatisfaction of the opposition parties, which believed that the winning party had been fraudulently elected. In protest, the Lesotho Defense Force (LDF) seized arms and ammunition and expelled or imprisoned their commanding officers. Government vehicles were hijacked, the broadcasting station was closed, and the prime minister and other ministers were virtually held hostage as the Lesotho police lost control of the situation.

News about the coup spread, triggering rumors of potential regional intervention even before Operation Boleas was launched in September 1998. In SADC's military invasion into Lesotho, led by South Africa's South African National Defence Force (SANDF),[37] approximately 600 South African troops were joined by approximately 200 troops from the Botswana Defense Force (BDF) and several local troops, in an attempt to enforce law and order in chaotic

36 *Ibid.*, 29–30.

37 Tavares, "The Participation of SADC and ECOWAS in Military Operations: The Weight of National Interests in Decision-Making," 158–61.

post-election Lesotho. On ground, however, SADC's inexperience in missions of this type caused the escalation of the situation.

In the ensuing debate over the legitimacy of the operation, Operation Boleas was accused of being more strongly driven by South African, rather than regional, interests. Critics claimed that South Africa's decision to intervene was driven by its stake in the Lesotho Highlands Water Project (LHWP), an ongoing water supply project of Lesotho and South Africa, which was at the time Africa's largest water transfer scheme, and by South Africa's fears of the conflict's spillover into its own territory, for example by a large influx of refugees.[38] Critics also stated that the SADC's mandate to intervene in Lesotho's internal affairs was not clearly defined, the decision to intervene had not been ratified by the SADC Summit, and that it was, in general, a much more "South African mission" than "SADC mission".[39]

The legitimacy of intervention in other states' affairs, particularly when intervention includes military action and involves a regional power or a strong state in the affairs of a weaker state, remained a major dilemma in the future of regional interventions. Debates on related issues – such as whether to respond to a military intervention by a member state of a regional organization in its neighboring state before the regional organization decides on the agreed methods of intervention – re-emerged, for example, in the case of the Ugandan military intervention in South Sudan and IGAD's ambivalent attitudes toward Ugandan action, as discussed in the following chapters.

Another crisis that required SADC's attention was the second phase of the DRC civil war, which spiraled into what is considered the deadliest war after World War II, with an estimated death toll of 5.4 million. While an account of the numerous political, economic, and other factors responsible for the outbreak and the escalation of the second phase in the civil war in Democratic Republic of Congo (1998–2003)[40] is beyond the scope of this book, the regional aspects of the DRC conflict should be mentioned, as they are relevant to the regional perspective of this book. First, the outbreak of the conflict was clearly related to regional developments. Although the conflict was referred to as a "war of liberation" from the prolonged dictatorship of Mobutu Sese Seko (1991–1997), many internal aspirations and tension were fueled by the interests of DRC's neighbors and specifically by the developments in Rwanda. In many

38 *Ibid.*

39 Johnson, "The 1998 Military Intervention in Lesotho: SADC Peace Mission or Resource War?"

40 See, for example: *Coltan, Congo and conflict: Polinares Case Study*; Prunier, *Africa's World War: Congo, the Rwanda Genocide, and the Making of a Continental Catastrophe*, 9.

respects, the DRC civil war is considered to be its continuation, with the same belligerents fighting in different territories. In the first phase of the war, the Rwandan Hutu militia forces, commonly known as Interahamwe, used the Hutu refugee camps in eastern Zaire.[41] A coalition of Rwandan and Ugandan armies invaded Zaire, assumed control of several mineral mining sites, and proceeded to attack the Hutu militia and overthrow Mobutu's government, in support of the Alliance des Forces démocratiques pour la libération du Congo (AFDL), a coalition of opposition parties led by Laurent-Désiré Kabila. However, once installed in power, the new President Kabila (1997–2001) invested greater efforts in forging new clientelism networks than in promoting a genuine democratic transition. The second and brutal phase of the DRC civil war erupted almost immediately, and the country became almost equally split between the government and the rebel forces.

Second, the deteriorating situation on the ground and Kabila's weak regime propelled him to appeal to outside intervention for assistance in responding to the rebel attacks: In June 1999, the belligerents in the DRC[42] met in Lusaka, Zambia, together with mediators and observers from SADC, OAU, and the UN, and signed the Lusaka agreement one month later. SADC played a more marginal role in the process than did the OAU, but SADC continued to expand its intervention in the DRC, in line with the interests of the countries of the region: The DRC, a huge country and one of the most resource-rich countries in the continent, was considered a much more interesting target for SADC's member states. Just as the decision on military intervention in Lesotho had been driven mainly by South Africa, the decision to intervene militarily in the DRC was also driven mainly by one member state, in this case Zimbabwe. Zimbabwean President Robert Mugabe, concerned by the increasing involvement of Rwanda, Uganda, and Burundi, and their aspirations to establish their own spheres of security interests in the DRC, was tempted to play an active role in the developments in the DRC. In many respects, this intervention reflected the complex relations between the member states and their diverging and sometimes conflicting interests. One of the preliminary clues to this complexity was

41 Zaire is the DRC's former name under the rule of Mobutu Sese Seko (1971–1997).

42 Kabila's AFDL (Alliance of Democratic Forces for the Liberation of Congo) was brought together by Rwanda and its allies to act as a front for its invasion of Zaire. The Alliance brought together four disparate movements: The Democratic People's Alliance (DPA), consisting mainly of Zairean Tutsi – the Banyamulenge who were fighting for their right to citizenship and led by Deogratias Bugera; the Revolutionary Movement for the Liberation of Zaire led by Anselme Masasu Nindanga; The National Resistance Council for Democracy led by André Kisase Ngandu from Kasai who became the first leader and commander of the AFDL forces; and the People's Revolutionary Party.

the fact that the military intervention in the DRC was only retroactively recognized by SADC.[43]

Third, according to Tavares, "The DRC conflict also showed clearly how national and personal interests become intertwined."[44] As with intervention in Lesotho, Zimbabwe launched a massive military intervention in the DRC with approximately 10,000 troops and an annual investment of approximately USD 36 million (between 1998 and 2002),which created a heavy burden for the already struggling Zimbabwean economy. The motives for this large-scale intervention were diverse. Mugabe, the national leader of the struggle against the white-minority rule in Rhodesia in the 1970s, was threatened by the rising star of Nelson Mandela's South Africa, and sought drastic and heroic moves to recover his personal and national prestige. Indeed, in many respects, it could be claimed that Zimbabwe, and to a lesser scope, Angola, were trying to challenge South Africa's aspirations through their intervention in the DRC conflict. More importantly, Mugabe sought to secure the economic benefits that were generated by the personal ties between the elites of the two countries. For example, Zimbabwe acquired two of the richest state-owned mining concessions in the DRC, and in return provided many, including financial, benefits to DRC companies and well-connected individuals.[45] Economic benefits based on personal ties also motivated other SADC member states, such as Angola and Namibia, to intervene in the DRC.

Nonetheless, the claim that SADC failed to become a forum to reduce uncertainly, monitor compliance, and detect defections[46] ignores the successful aspects of SADC's intervention in the DRC, such as its mediation and peacemaking efforts, which resulted in the signing of the DRC's Global and All-Inclusive Agreement in December 2002.[47] This agreement was one of the crucial initiatives that led to the resolution of the DRC conflict after the collapse of the Lusaka Ceasefire Agreement signed in July 1999. The efforts to find a durable solution included dialogue with participants other than the official belligerents in the war, namely the Kabila government, the rebel movements, and the external armed forces. South Africa also hosted the Inter-Congolese

43 Tavares, "The Participation of SADC and ECOWAS in Military Operations: The Weight of National Interests in Decision-Making," 158–61.

44 *Ibid.*, 165.

45 There is evidence, for instance, of personal economic relations between Joseph Kabila (Kabila's son) and Leo Mugabe (Mugabe's nephew). See *ibid.*, 163 and also: Nzongola-Ntalaja, "Civil war, Peacekeeping and the Great Lakes Region."

46 Tavares, "The Participation of SADC and ECOWAS in Military Operations," 165–6.

47 SADC, "Global and Inclusive Agreement on Transition in the Democratic Republic of the Congo."

Dialogue for the DRC.[48] The inclusion of unarmed Congolese actors who had been previously excluded from peacemaking efforts conveyed an important message, acknowledging that mediation and peace-building processes should include other factions of the society beside the warlords, in order to create agreements that include future power-sharing in the post-conflict society.

The complexity of ECOWAS missions in Liberia, Sierra Leone, and Guinea-Bissau thus created numerous challenges for its members, such as the need to secure in advance a clear mandate for intervention from both regional and international organizations, and sufficient financial, intelligence, military, and logistical resources for the military intervention. On the brighter side, lessons from the West African interventions indicated that in some cases, even in cases of continuing and serious conflicts, a multiplicity of mediators could contribute to success of the negotiations. SADC's mediation efforts and actions, such as the imposition of sanctions and embargos on the DRC, were helpful in facilitating the peace-building process there and demonstrated the organization's abilities to bring to an end one of the severest conflicts in post-Cold War Africa. SADC continued to play a leading role in the peace process until the establishment of a new transitional government of national unity in the DRC in July 2003, although the transition from state of war to a period of peace-building was far from concluded: Violence continues and peace agreements remain fragile to the present. Foreign interests continue to play a dominant role in the DRC, and neighboring countries, such as Rwanda and Uganda, continue to maintain troops in the DRC, and regional, continental, and international exploitation of its national resources continues as well. These issues are discussed with reference to IGAD's mediation efforts in the following chapters.

•••

At the turn of the century, despite the limitations and setbacks of the regional interventions, a new commitment to engage in more effective regional interventions in the continent's conflicts emerged. This commitment was related to the personal agendas of two prominent African leaders: South African President Thabo Mbeki (1999–2008) and Nigerian President Olusegun Obasanjo (1999–2007). Both leaders condemned African adherence to the principles of the sovereignty and nonintervention in the internal affairs of the states, and advocated a new interventionist stance, promising to create an area of peacekeeping.[49]

48 Adedajo and Landsberg, "South Africa and Nigeria as Regional Hegemons," 189.

49 Adedajo and Landsberg, "The Heirs of Nkrumah: Africa's New Interventionists." For a detailed discussion in the issue of the changes in African discourse on these issues, see:

By the end of the 1990s, in addition to their efforts to strengthen institutional ties between ECOAWS and SADC, Obasanjo and Mbeki also promoted the idea of a new security architecture for Africa. For example, "they championed the idea of military intervention by regional bodies in four specific cases: first, to reverse an unconstitutional change of regimes; second, to prevent genocide; third, in cases of instability that threaten to spread to engulf other states; and forth, under gross violations of human rights."[50] The two presidents' new commitment reflected a broader continental shift in attitudes toward regional organizations' role in intervening and preventing conflicts in the stormy environment of post-Cold War Africa.

The lessons learned from previous interventions were assimilated into the broader conception of Africa Peace and Security Architecture that was being developed at the time and resulted in the establishment of the African Union (AU) in 2002 and its Peace and Security Council (PCS). The guiding principles of the new security and peacekeeping organization were grounded in the longstanding commitment to principles such as respect for territorial integrity, sanctity of boundaries, and non-interference; but also offered more concrete definitions for prevention and reduction of intra-state conflicts, including "increase in human rights violations in a polity."[51]

In contrast to the OAU's vague commitment to the principle of "peaceful dispute settlement," the AU seemed to have added checks and balances and other monitoring mechanisms that potentially made it a "more effective, democratic, and autonomous organization."[52] Moreover, on the issue of intervention in intrastate conflicts, Article 4(h) of the Constitutive Act defined "the right of the Union to intervene in a member state pursuant to a decision of the Assembly in respect of grave circumstances, namely war crimes, genocide and crimes against humanity."[53] The PSC was established to coordinate all responses to events involving grave human rights violations, and ultimately prevent, control, and resolve conflicts in the continent.

As for the coordination between continental and regional levels, a framework guiding the relationship between the AU and Regional Economic

---

Back, *Intervention and Sovereignty in Africa: Conflict Resolution and International Organizations in Darfur*.

50 Adedajo and Landsberg, "The Heirs of Nkrumah."

51 African Union, Report on the Status of the Establishment of the Continental Peace and Security Architecture. See also: Engel and Gomes Porto, *Africa's New Peace and Security Architecture, Promoting Norms, Institutionalizing Solutions*, 212–17.

52 Zweifel, *International Organizations and Democracy: Accountability, Politics, and Power*, 148.

53 African Union, Constitutive Act of the African Union, Article 4(h).

Communities (RECs) was defined in the Protocol on Relations between the AU and RECs, adopted in July 2007 in Accra, Ghana. The RECs have been central to various transformative programs on the continent, including the New Partnership for Africa's Development (NEPAD) adopted in 2001, and have played a major role in development and economic progress as well as peace and security, tackling the immense tasks of working with governments, civil society, and the AU Commission to prevent conflicts and initiate peace-building processes.[54]

As this chapter reveals, regional African organizations became increasingly involved in mediation efforts, peacekeeping trials, and even direct intervention in intrastate conflicts in the post-Cold War era. The reasons for the increasing involvement were varied and included growing belief in the perception of "African solutions to African problems," concerns about the spillover effects of intrastate conflicts and the threats they pose to regional stability, as well as the political, economic, or personal interests of the interveners. Most of the interventions described in this chapter were concentrated in the western and southern regions of the continent, areas that have attracted most of the literature's attention. The following chapter focuses on the eastern region of the continent, and more precisely, on the efforts of a regional organization, IGAD, to mediate in the conflicts in Sudan and South Sudan. In the final chapter of the book, however, we return to a comparative continental approach to analyze IGAD's achievements and setbacks since the turn of the century.

54 UN, "The Regional Economic Communities (RECs) of the African Union."

CHAPTER 2

From Ecology to Mediation: IGAD's First Steps as a Regional Mediator

During the first half of the 1980s, Nigeria's commitment to ECOWAS was on the wane. Despite the Nigerian state's efforts to establish the regional organization and protect its influence, Nigeria repeatedly violated its commitments to ECOWAS. In January 1983, in stark contrast to the 1979 ECOWAS Protocol on the Free Movement of Persons, which Nigeria had signed, Nigerian authorities expelled two million non-Nigerian ECOWAS citizens, claiming they were "illegal aliens," an act that probably expressed Nigerian leadership's desire to sacrifice aspirations of regional integration on the altar of xenophobic nationalism.[1] With the rise to power of Ibrahim Babaginda in 1985, however, Nigeria's authorities demonstrated a renewed commitment to the regional organization, including a large investment in building a new ECOWAS secretariat in Abuja, Nigeria's new capital. The connection between the country's actions and its efforts to make peace in Sudan, located on the far side of the continent, was subsequently revealed when Babaginda was nominated OAU's chairman. Wearing his new hat, he continued to prove ECOWAS's commitment to conflict resolution with a continental-broad perspective when he initiated two rounds of talks between the rival factions of Sudan that took place in Abuja in 1992 and 1993.[2] These talks also mark the beginnings of IGADD's involvement in the mediation process. This chapter begins with a brief description of the causes of the second phase of the Sudanese civil war (1983–2005) and its main developments.

The civil war between the deprived South and the politically dominant North erupted even before the British ceded colonial control in 1955, and continued uninterrupted until 1972, when the first phase of the war ended. The roots of the South's sense of deprivation stemmed from the longstanding socio-economic implications of Sudan's state-building processes, such as the neglect of the periphery. The *Jellaba,* whose origins can be traced to the Nile

1 Adebajo, *Building Peace in West Africa: Liberia, Sierra Leone, and Guinea-Bissau,* 33–4.

2 For a detailed analysis of the Abuja talks, see Wöndu and Lesch, *Battle for Peace in Sudan: An Analysis of the Abuja Conferences, 1992–1993.*

 | DOI:10.1163/9789004425323_004

Valley,[3] were a thriving class of wealthy merchants and officials at the time of the Turko-Egyptian conquest in the nineteenth century, and they continued to prosper under British colonial rule. Through the British colonial system, the *Jellaba* created networks of political and economic alliances with British officials and traditional rulers, resulting in the spread of this elite group into the southern, eastern, and western districts of the colony. As a result, the *Jellaba* were better prepared to inherit political and state power in 1956. As a result of the *Jellaba*'s dominant Nilo-centrist and Arab supremacist ideology, Arabic became the language of instruction in schools and Islamism became the state ideology after independence.[4]

In the first phase of Sudanese civil war, persistent impoverishment and underdevelopment of the South were exacerbated by chronic political instability in Sudan's political center.[5] Although a cease-fire accord between the Sudanese government and the leaders of the rebellious south was signed under the autocratic military rule of Ja'afr al-Nimeiri (1969–1985), and the South was guaranteed some degree of autonomy under the terms of the 1972 Addis Ababa Agreement, it soon became apparent that the government of Khartoum would not fulfill its promises to the South, for several reasons, primarily its desire to control the oil reserves in the South.

Oil exploration, which had not been highly relevant when the Addis Ababa Agreement was signed in 1972, become much more important in the late 1970s and early 1980s.[6] Oil exploration drove efforts to demarcate the north-south border (an issue that remains unresolved to thc present, as elaborated below). A manifestation of Khartoum's intentions was its increasing intervention in the political affairs of the south, and particularly the imposition of strict religious ideologies in the form of laws. In June 1983, President Nimeiri announced his promulgation of Republican Order Number One, which split the southern Regional Assembly of Juba into three weaker administrative units, and substituted Arabic for English (to name only a few violations of the 1972 Agreement). Worse, in September that year, the ruling party imposed *sharī'a* law on all people and provinces of Sudan. This act, which became commonly known as "the September Laws," was considered the catalyst for the eruption of the Second Civil War between the North and the South that year, which continued

3 For the origins and historical development of this community see: McHugh, *Holy men of the Blue Nile: the Making of an Arab-Islamic Community in the Nilotic Sudan, 1500–1850*.

4 Rolandsen and Daly, *A History of South Sudan: From Slavery to Independence*, 1–79.

5 Poggo, *The First Sudanese Civil War: Africans, Arabs, and Israelis in the Southern Sudan, 1955–1972*.

6 Patey, "Crude Days Ahead? Oil and the Resource Curse in Sudan," 619–20.

until 2005[7] to become what is considered post-colonial Africa's longest civil war, accounting for approximately two million deaths and four million refugees and IDPs.[8]

It was, however, not long after the proclamation of the September Laws that a glimmer of hope of rapprochement between the South and the North emerged. In March 1985, a popular rising (*intifada*) in the streets of Khartoum, led by a group called National Alliance for National Salvation, called for the restoration of democracy in Sudan, and eventually led to the overthrow of President Nimeiri. Encouraged by this development, the Sudan People's Liberation Movement in Opposition (SPLM-IO), which by that time had achieved some military victories in the South, sought to bring as many parties as possible to the negotiation table. In March 1986, delegations of the SPLM-IO and the National Alliance met in a convention in Koka Dam in Ethiopia to discuss: (a) a declaration by all political forces and the government of the day of their commitment to discuss "the Basic Problems of Sudan" and not the so-called problem of southern Sudan; (b) lifting of the State of Emergency; (c) repeal of the September 1983 Laws and all other liberty-restricting laws; and (d) adoption of the 1956 Constitution as amended in 1964, including reference to the incorporation of "regional governments," and all other matters on which a consensus of all the political forces would be reached.[9]

Hope for rapprochement between the North and the South quickly faded during the convention itself. The implications of the absence of two of the major Northern parties, the Democratic Unionist Party (DUP) and the National Islamic Front (NIF), were revealed one year later, when general elections were held in Sudan. Sadiq al-Mahdi, Chairman of the winning *Umma* party and President-elect, announced that he was dropping out of the Koka Dam agreements, which his party's predecessor had signed. When efforts to reconcile the new elected government and the Southern leaders failed, the conflict on the ground escalated once again.[10] It was against this backdrop that the Sudanese government made its initial application to the fledgling organization of IGADD,

7 Shinn, "Addis Ababa Agreement: Was it Destined to Fail and are There Lessons for the Current Sudan Peace Process?"

8 For a detailed description of the roots and development of Sudan civil war, see: [*The*] *Anya-Nya Struggle: Background and Objectives*; Collins, *Civil Wars and Revolution in the Sudan: Essays on the Sudan, Southern Sudan, and Darfur, 1962–2004*; Rolandsen and Daly, *A History of South Sudan: From Slavery to Independence*, 93–132.

9 IGAD, "Koka Dam Declaration"; See also: Garang and Khālid, *The Call for Democracy in Sudan*, 112–44.

10 Johnson, *The Root Causes of Sudan's Civil Wars*, 70–2.

requesting mediation in March 1988.[11] To understand why it applied to an organization that was originally established as a regional environmental organization, a brief description of the IGADD's establishment and early history is required.

The establishment of the regional organization Inter-Governmental Authority on Draught and Development (IGADD) had been motivated primarily by environmental reasons. The decade between 1974 and 1984 was characterized by a series of ecological disasters including severe recurring draughts and waves of famine.[12] The six founding member-states of the organization, Djibouti, Ethiopia, Kenya, Somalia, Sudan, and Uganda,[13] shared many common vulnerabilities, including 80% arid and semi-arid lowland, and more than half of the population under 14 years old.[14] After almost three years of negotiations, the six East African states acted through the United Nations Environmental Programme (UNEP) to establish the organization. In January 1986, the secretariat headquarters of IGADD was officially inaugurated in Djibouti.

IGADD's initial objectives and functions focused on ecological crises and related issues such as food security.[15] The founding documents of IGADD were limited to environmental cooperation and included no reference to political or security issues. Although "the absence of a security mandate was not accidental or an oversight but rather a deliberate decision that resulted from a domestic politics of the member countries, intra-state conflicts and an unfavorable international environment for meaningful security cooperation," it quickly emerged that the complex geopolitical characteristics of the region could not be ignored:

> State borders divide communities nearly everywhere in the IGAD region, making it likely that even localized conflicts can have broader dimensions and complications. Nearly all state borders lines in the region pass through pastoralist areas, obscuring the natural movement of people, livestock and trade. Conflict involving communities can spill over frontier lines when help is sought from kinsmen across the border, or when it offers a handy sanctuary. Raiding for animals, a widespread practice in

11 Yihun, "Ethiopia's Role in South Sudan's March to Independence, 1955–1991," 45.

12 These environmental changes elicited an international response in the form of the 1992 Rio UN Summit, which led to the UN Convention to Combat Desertification, considered a pioneering step toward establishing international environmental law.

13 Eritrea, the seventh member of the organization, joined after its independence in 1993.

14 "The Inter-Governmental Authority on Drought and Development (IGADD)," 93.

15 Hubbard et al., "Regional Food Security Strategies: The Case of IGADD in the Horn of Africa."

> pastoralist zone, often takes place across borders. Commercialization of livestock and animal products plus accessing to automatic weapons has greatly raised the stakes in this practice, occasionally resulting in what might be termed intra state incidents.[16]

Recognition of the inseparable interwoven nature of environmental, political, and security issues evolved particularly in the case of South Sudan.[17] The newborn IGADD was yet unprepared to deal effectively with the vast complexities of the Sudanese civil war, and the failure of its first mediation efforts is not surprising. Nonetheless, these efforts (described below) turned out to be the spearhead of its ongoing role as mediator in Sudan.[18]

The democratic phase of the Sudanese state, described above, was short lived. A wave of violence erupted in response to the country's 1989 Islamic revolution, which was accompanied with the imposition of fierce Islamist ideology throughout the country, including the predominantly Christian south.[19] Shortly after the National Islamic Front (NIF) seized power in Sudan, it became evident that the clash between the Islamist and Arab supremacist ideology of the ruling party and the SPLM/A's demands for secularism and equality reached a boiling point, as described by Gen. Lazaro Sumbeiywo, who was later Kenya's Special Envoy to IGAD:

> Motivated by what he saw as *jihad*, the army vowed not to give up any inch of the soil to the Africans and government officials rushed to their allies abroad to plead for assistance for what they called "winning back Arab towns captured by Africans infidels." On the other hand, Garang and the SPLM/A refused to recognize Bashir as President because the military coup that brought him to power had ousted a democratically elected leader, Mahdi, and they denounced the military junta as "running dogs of Islamic fundamentalism."[20]

Mounting tensions between the rival parties triggered a call for renewed mediation efforts, which came in a context of major global and continental

16 Berhe. "Regional Peace and Security Cooperation under the Intergovernmental Authority on Development: Development and Challenges," 108.

17 The Inter-Governmental Authority on Drought and Development (IGADD), 93.

18 El-Effendi, "The Impasse in the IGAD Peace Process for Sudan: The Limits of Regional Peacemaking."

19 Natsios, *Sudan, South Sudan, and Darfur: What Everyone Needs to Know*, 80–113.

20 Waihenya, *The Mediator. Gen. Lazaro Sumbeiywo and the Southern Sudan Peace Process*, 70–1. This book is discussed extensively in the following chapters.

changes. The request for mediation also came at a time of significant regional change: The emergence of the second wave of regional functional organizations, backed by international support, marked a shift from the concept of "African solutions to African problems" to "African sub-regional solutions to African sub-regional problems," and changing relations between Africa's continental and sub-regional organizations.[21] During the 1990s, the Organization of African Unity (OAU) remained largely committed to the principle of non-intervention in the internal affairs of the sovereign states, and therefore took a very cautious stand. It was conceivable that this vacuum would be filled by the regional organizations of Africa, as the following case illustrates.

In the early 1990s, under an OAU mandate, Ibrahim Babaginda, then Nigerian president and OAU chair, initiated two rounds of talks in in 1992 and 1993 in Abuja – one of the mediation teams included a group from IGADD.[22] Although the efforts to create a dialogue between the rival parties ultimately failed, some features of this initial mediation effort have particular significance, as they came to characterize future mediation efforts of IGADD (and IGAD).

One of the most prominent features of the 1992–1993 Abuja talks was the adoption of the "African solutions to African problems" concept, which implied more active involvement of African continental and regional organizations in internal conflicts of their member states. This concept was embraced by Babaginda, who, as the chair of the continental organization, wished to demonstrate a more active stance toward intervention in intrastate conflicts, and also to combine forces with the mediation efforts of other regional organizations. Al-Bashir stated that "Babaginda is the logical mediator because of his sincerity on issues concerning the African continent, Nigeria's experience in solving problems of internal conflict, as well as the fact that he is the current OAU Chairman."[23] The argument that African countries and communities shared many historical similarities and common practices of mediation was raised repeatedly over the course of the protracted mediation efforts between the North and the South in Sudan.

Another lesson to be learned from the Abuja talks is that the mediation process had to consider the multiple parties involved in the conflict and

21 Adar "Conflict Resolution in a Turbulent Region: The Case of the Intergovernmental Authority on Development (IGAD) in Sudan," 42–3.

22 See: Wondu and Lesch, *Battle for Peace in Sudan: An Analysis of the Abuja Conferences 1992–93*; Back, *Intervention and Sovereignty in Africa: Conflict Resolution and International Organisations in Darfur*, 80–1; Johnson, *The Root Causes of Sudan's Civil Wars*.

23 Cited in: Khadiagala, *Meddlers or Mediators? African Interveners in Civil Conflicts in Eastern Africa*, 190.

their complicated relations: major rival parties were themselves split into sub-groups, with their own rivalries, coalitions, and interests. According to Rupesinghe, it is important to identify all the actors of the conflict, irrespective of their political weight, bring them to the negotiating table, and take into account the opinion of each of them. Failure to bring all the actors into the peace process can result in a breakdown of the process.[24]

In fact, mapping the internal splits and understanding their roots and dynamics are crucially important for understanding future developments including the present conflict in South Sudan and IGAD's mediation efforts there. The National Islamic Front (NIF) itself was divided into at least two main factions (Al-Bashir supporters and al-Turabi supporters), and also faced fierce Northern opposition, as will be elaborated below.[25] The case with the SPLA was even more complicated: Three of the movement's commanders, Riek Machar, Lam Kol, and Gordon Kong, sought to depose the movement's leader, John Garang. When their efforts failed, they created a new faction – SPLA-Nasir. The split in the SPLA was motivated by ethnic, political, ideological, and external reasons. The main rivalry in the movement involved two dominant ethnic groups, the Dinka and the Nuer, although many others ethnic groups were struggling to find their place within the movement.[26] The three dissidents also preferred the political solution of southern secession, which challenged Garang's view of New Sudan (elaborated below). Moreover, the internal clashes in the SPLA were encouraged, or even created to some degree, by Northern politicians.

However, it was not the internal splits in the SPLA that led to the collapse of the first round of the Abuja talks, but rather the parties' inability to agree on core issues, such as secularism, the future relationship between the North and the South, and interim agreements.[27] Although Kenyan and Ugandan leaders, at the behest of the Sudanese government, persuaded the rival parties to return to the negotiating table after the talks collapsed, gaps between the negotiating parties remained even after the second round of Abuja talks in April 1993.[28] Meanwhile, on the ground, the civil war escalated, and a mass famine threatened the area of the Upper Nile and Bahr el Ghazal that became known as "Starvation Triangle."[29] This situation attracted the attention of international actors including the UN and the United States, which began to recognize that preventing further aggravation of the humanitarian situation

24 Rupesinghe, *Conflict Transformation*, 167.
25 See, for example: Natsios, *Sudan, South Sudan, and Darfur*, 80–98.
26 Khadiagala, *Meddlers or Mediators:* 190.
27 Wondu and Lesch, *Battle for Peace in Sudan*, 65.
28 *Ibid.*, 96–119.
29 Khadiagala, *Meddlers or Mediators*, 191.

required a resolution of the Sudanese conflict. After efforts to identify potential local mediators, they subsequently appealed to IGADD to lead the mediation process.[30]

By 1993, IGADD had already achieved several diplomatic successes, such as its initiative to re-establish diplomatic relations between the former bitter rivals Ethiopia and Somalia.[31] More than its growing experience, it was the ongoing and escalating conflict in Sudan, with its regionally destabilizing effects, that spurred the organization to assume a more active role in conflict mediation and prevention, as El-Effendi observed: "The motive of IGADD leaders in taking the task of the mediation was first to integrate and contain Khartoum in the interest of regional stability."[32] Indeed, Sudan's central position in the region, and its continuous, devastating civil war, compelled IGADD to intensify its mediation efforts. At this point it is interesting to explore the conflicting parties' motives to join the mediation process proposed by the regional organization, as well as the motives of the member states themselves.

Since the Islamist revolution of 1989, Sudan had faced increasing regional and international isolation. From the outset, the revolution, whose ideological underpinnings were supplied by Hasan al-Turabi, was accompanied by internal struggles for dominance within the ruling NIF, especially between Turabi and Omar al-Bashir. It soon became clear that al-Bashir was the dominant force in the NIF party, and that the new party sought to maintain the established order of Northern-Islamic hegemony over the entire country, including the predominantly Christian south. Moreover, the support of Khartoum's Islamist regime to extremist groups, including hosting Osama Bin Laden in Sudan (1991–1996), and its alleged support of terror attacks against Western targets, reinforced Western, particularly US, recognition of the South as a potential ally of the West.[33] The support by the Sudanese government of Iraq's invention to Kuwait alienated many of Sudan's traditional allies, including the oil-rich Gulf States and several Arab League states such as Egypt, Tunisia, and Algeria.[34] Many of Sudan's neighbors, including IGADD members, such as Ethiopia, Kenya, and Uganda, which are pre-dominantly Christian but have substantial Muslim minorities, shared concerns of the destabilizing regional effects of the Sudanese Islamist revolution, and their leaders tended to strengthen their

30 Iyob and Khadiagala, *Sudan: The Elusive Quest for Peace*, 101–32; El-Effendi, "The Impasse in the IGAD Peace Process for Sudan: The Limits of Regional Peacemaking."

31 Adar, "Conflict Resolution in a Turbulent Region," 46–7.

32 El-Effendi, "The Impasse in the IGAD Peace Process for Sudan," 589.

33 Ylönen, "Security Regionalism and Flaws of Externally Forged Peace in Sudan: The IGAD Peace Process and its Aftermath," 20–2.

34 Khadiagala, *Meddlers or Mediators*, 193.

support of the South. Al-Bashir's suspicions of a Western-Christian conspiracy to topple his regime were not unfounded, as since the first phase of the civil war, support of the South had consolidated along lines of religious affiliation. As Johnson claims, "Government-sponsored construction of mosques and religious schools throughout South Sudan and the expulsion of Christian missionaries in 1964 convinced South Sudanese of the government's hostility to Christianity, and both the Anyanya and the SPLA/M received support from church groups."[35]

The support of various Christian organizations in the South was, in many cases, followed by penetration of humanitarian organizations that viewed the Northern regime's actions in the South as kind of neo-colonialist intervention in the internal affairs of the [South] Sudanese state. Fearing that humanitarian intervention would be followed by penetration of Western states and organizations, al-Bashir preferred regional rather than international intervention, claiming that it "would be neutral without loopholes through which colonialism could penetrate on the pretext of humanitarianism."[36]

Southern leaders were concerned by IGADD's disposition toward the al-Bashir government, but the SPLM/A had several reasons for joining the process. One was the recognition of its inability to achieve a military victory; the second was economic. Due to the discovery of significant reserves of oil in the 1990s, Khartoum strengthened its commercial ties with non-Western powers, primarily China, and purchased copious amounts of weaponry. These economic and military capabilities allowed the Government of Sudan (GoS) to support regional groups that were combating against the South, and even to indirectly encourage the ethnic split within the South itself. Indeed, the conflict between the Dinka and the Nuer, which had split the SPLM/A since 1991, was the main cause of the drastic deterioration in humanitarian conditions, which claimed over 20,000 lives in 1991–1993 and was a main obstacle to consolidation of a unified Southern front.[37] The deterioration of the situation in the South persuaded Garang to accept IGADD's mediation offer, not without expressing its own reservations:

35 The Anya-Nya Struggle: Background and Objectives; Johnson, *South Sudan: A New History for a New Nation*, 147. See also the declaration from World Council of Churches' (WCC) meeting in Harare, Zimbabwe, cited in Adar, "Conflict Resolution in a Turbulent Region," 54.

36 Apuuli Phillip, "IGAD's Mediation in the Current South Sudan Conflict: Prospects and Challenges," 126.

37 Following a grassroots church-led peace initiative in 1999, a local peace agreement known as the Wunlit Dinka-Nuer Covenant was signed, which strengthened the SPLM's ability to negotiate with the GoS as a single united movement. See: Adar, "Conflict Resolution in a Turbulent Region," 55–6.

> I expect a lot from these states because they are our neighbors and the sense they are affected by our problem whether through the exodus of refugees or instability on the borders. Some of these states, like Eritrea and Ethiopia, are on good terms with Khartoum. True, they treat us as rebels and treat the Khartoum government as a government, but there is no other way. So long as the Khartoum government and the two wings of the Sudanese people's Movement have accepted the initiative, the chances of making progress seem to be good.[38]

One reason for the Sudanese government's willingness to accept IGADD's renewed mediation efforts was based on its assumption that two of the organization's members, Ethiopia and Eritrea, owe to Sudan an historical debt due to its support in their own revolutions.[39] Yet, it soon turned out that both countries were apprehensive about the Islamic radicalism of the Sudanese regime, and Ethiopia even blamed Sudan for involvement in the assassination attempt of Egyptian President Hosni Mubarak during his visit in Ethiopia in 1995. Uganda was also joining the two other IGADD members in their opposition to the GoS ideological and political stances, and in practice were supporting the SPLM/A, while encouraging its alliance with the northern opposition parties' NDA.[40]

IGADD established a mediation committee composed of the presidents of Kenya, Uganda, Eritrea, and Ethiopia, with Kenyan President Daniel Arap Moi as its chair. IGADD convened four rounds of talks during 1993–1994, with the participation of representatives of the GoS and the two factions of the SPLM. The difference in the positions of the rival parties, and especially the tough positions of the GoS representatives, drove this round of talks into a dead-end. Instead of dealing with the main issues, such as self-determination or the conditions for a cease-fire, the parties reached an agreement only on relatively marginal issues such as open-air corridors, land passages, and immunization of children living in the war zone.[41]

In March 1994 another round of negotiations began in Nairobi, ending with the presentation of the Declaration of Principles (DoP), which included

---

38 Cited in: Khadiagala, *Meddlers or Mediators*, 195.

39 While they were fighting against Mengistu regime, Sudan provided sanctuary for the former allies, EPLF and EPRDF (former Tigray People Liberation Front-TPLF).

40 Johnson, *The Root Causes of Sudan's Civil Wars*, 102–3; Wöndu and Lesch, *Battle for Peace in Sudan*, 158–62.

41 Wöndu and Lesch, *Battle for Peace in Sudan*, 154.

recognition of the South's right to self-determination if the GoS failed to promote democratization, secularization, and regional equality.[42] In many ways, the DoP was similar to the principles agreed upon at the Koka Dam convention several years earlier. Similarly to that convention, the two Southern factions agreed to accept the principles, while Khartoum backed down, and the DoP was never effectively signed. Ghazi Salih al-Din, the GoS's militant representative to the negotiations, even cautioned participants of a possible domino effect, expressing the deepest fears of most post-colonial states in Africa: "Self-determination-alias-separation of southern Sudan is bound to elicit a chain-reaction afflicting the rest of Africa. This is eventually what the founding fathers of the OAU consciously tried to avoid."[43] But, as Johnson claimed, although the DoP was not signed, "The very existence of this widely-agreed set of principles on which peace could be based was to have a significant impact on the international community and, ultimately, on the Sudanese opposition."[44]

Although IGADD's mediation efforts in Sudan were challenged by multiple factors, including the large number of actors within Sudan and diversity of interests among IGADD members, the process was profoundly affected by IGADD's new insistence on acting as a regional mediator in the second half of the 1990s. During this period, IGADD was able to rally international, and particularly Western, support for its mediation efforts and other regional activities. A group named Friends of IGADD, which included Australia, Britain, Canada, Italy, Norway, and United States, was established to support the organization's mediation efforts. Moreover, American support of the Southern cause grew under the Clinton administration; especially as the Northern government was considered a supporter of terrorism. The image of IGADD as an organization supported by the West intimidated the GoS, which requested that additional states, including South Africa, Zimbabwe, and later Egypt and Libya, participate in the mediation efforts.[45] On their part, Southern leaders sometime blamed IGADD for having pro-Northern tendencies. Yet, in spite of their mutual accusations of IGADD's biases, the rivals tended to admit that the organization was much more balanced than the alternative of no mediation and escalation of the conflict on ground, which had had devastating effects on both the North and the South (as described earlier).

IGADD's originally grandiose ambitions, such as those reflected in its 1992–1996 five-year program, were starkly contrasted with its severely limited

42 The IGAD Declaration of Principles, Nairobi, 20 May 1994.
43 Khadiagala, *Meddlers or Mediators*, 200–1.
44 Johnson, *The Root Causes of Sudan's Civil Wars*, 102.
45 Khadiagala, *Meddlers or Mediators*, 208–14.

operational capabilities: For example, its secretariat had only twelve professionals with no significant operational capabilities[46] and a very limited budget for mediation activities. Moreover, internal struggles of power between the member states seemed to undermine its abilities to mediate in the Sudanese conflict, as described by the well-known South Sudanese diplomat and scholar Francis Deng:

> Recent developments in the region, in particular the deterioration in bilateral relations between Sudan and two members of the IGADD mediation committee, Eritrea and Uganda (relations with Ethiopia and Kenya being more normal, if not entirely cordial), have made matters more complicated and threaten to undermine the effectiveness of the regional initiative. In both of these new bilateral disputes, each side has made incriminating allegations about subversive activities on the other's part, including recruiting, training, and the deployment of "terrorists" or "opposition forces" in border areas. Although Khartoum suspects all four committee members of sympathy for the south, Ethiopia and Kenya appear to have maintained postures more acceptable to Khartoum than those of Eritrea and Uganda.[47]

A name change was decided as one way to deal with the somewhat failed image of IGADD, with hopes that a new name would become associated with an image of a new, more effective organization. A round of intensive meetings and consultations in 1995–1996 between representatives of the member states, including ministers of foreign affairs, culminated in a summit in Nairobi in March 1995, where member states agreed to transform IGADD into IGAD, an organization with a new structure and an extended mandate.

The Agreement Establishing the Inter-Governmental Authority on Development (IGAD) reaffirmed its commitment to the sovereign equality of all member states and non-interference in the internal affairs of member states, while stressing a commitment to prevent, manage, and resolve inter- and intra-state conflicts through dialogue, as elaborated in Article 18A:

> Member States shall act collectively to preserve peace, security and stability which are essential prerequisites for economic development and social progress. Accordingly, Member States shall: (a) take effective

46 Weldesellassie, "IGAD as an International Organization, Its Institutional Development and Shortcomings," 3.

47 Deng, "Mediating the Sudanese Conflict: A Challenge for the IGADD," 7.

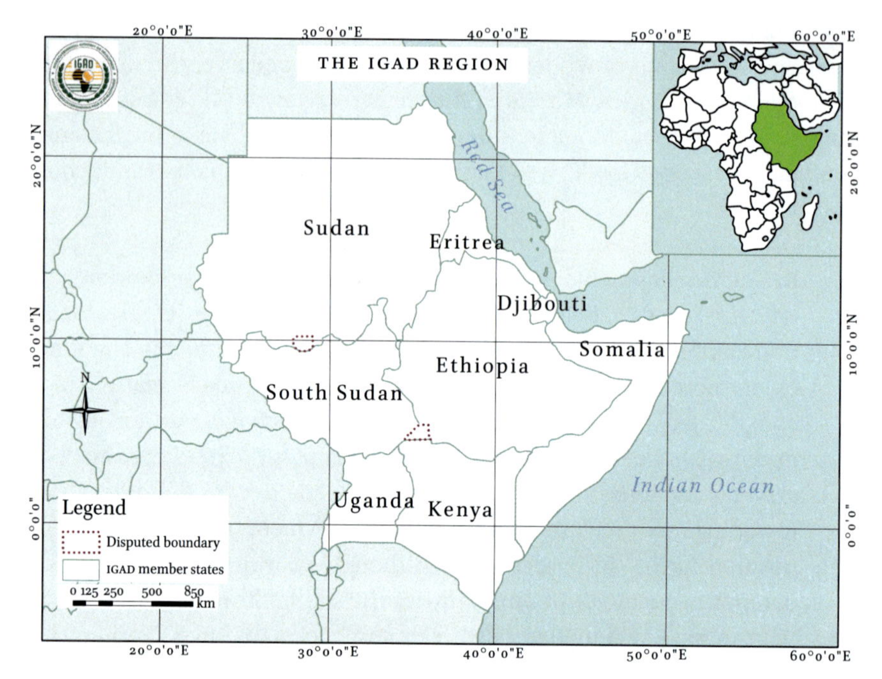

Map 1 Map of IGAD countries
Reference: Organ Bacteriological Dynamics in Heterobranchus bidorsalis juveniles fed diets fortified with Lactobacillus fermentum, Saccharomyces cerevisiae and their combination. Akanmu O A, Ajani E K, Omitoyin B O, Emikpe B Oand Ogunbanwo S T. - Scientific Figure On Researchgate. Available from: https://www.researchgate.net/figure/Map-of-IGAD-countries_fig1_315818798 [accessed 1 Mar, 2020.

> collective measures to eliminate threats to regional co-operation peace and stability; (b) establish an effective mechanism of consultation and cooperation for the pacific settlement of differences and disputes; (c) accept to deal with disputes between Member States within this sub-regional mechanism before they are referred to other regional or international organizations.[48]

The organization's transformation triggered a wave of optimism that was bolstered by the establishment of the IGAD Partners Forum (IPF), with representatives of Italy, Canada, and the UK, and chaired by Jan Pronk, Dutch Aid Minister and one of the co-presidents of the donor-government dialogue body, the Global Coalition for Africa. Compared to its predecessor (Friends of IGADD), the

48 Agreement Establishing the Inter-Governmental Authority on Development (IGAD), Nairobi, 21 March 1996.

Forum included many more states and international organizations.[49] In addition to the financial and political support that was guaranteed to IGAD by IPF, international organizations such as Amnesty International, Human Rights Watch, and UNHCHR proposed to station monitoring groups in the fighting area to monitor human rights. Renewed hope in IGAD's success was strengthened after al-Bashir agreed to return into the negotiating table with the SPLM/A, under IGAD's auspices, and surprisingly agreed to adopt the Declaration of Principles (DoP) as a starting point of the negotiations. Both the US and the EU agreed to donate funds to support IGAD's efforts. It soon emerged, however, that the Sudanese delegation slipped back into its rhetoric of Islamic supremacy and federalism without self-determination, and another round of talks ended without results.[50]

As the talks under the auspices of IGAD collapsed, the situation on the ground continued to deteriorate as famine struck in the spring of 1998 as a result of drought and warfare, threatening 350,000 southerners, and claiming over 100,000 lives.[51] IGAD foreign ministers met with the IPF in Rome in March 1998 to discuss whether humanitarian or political issues should be given priority, and agreed that a ceasefire was the most urgent goal at the time for humanitarian reasons.[52] The recurring waves of famine in South Sudan (and in other regions in Sudan; see below), raised a question of whether the organization should strengthen its initial commitment to focus with environmental deterioration and food security. The inability to reach effective resolutions on the organization's priorities in Rome was another sign of the setbacks that plagued the organization.

Stormy relations between the organization's members also hampered the effectiveness of IGAD's mediation efforts in this period. Hopes of new regional dynamics in the peace process were sparked when Eritrea became a member of IGAD in 1993, yet these hopes were shattered almost immediately in view of the deterioration in the relations between Eritrea and Sudan, both countries hurling mutual accusations: Eritrea accused Khartoum of supporting the Eritrean Islamic *jihad* and Sudan accused Asmara of the NDA, which was fighting against Bashir's regime.[53] Even worse, high hopes for full cooperation between Eritrea and Ethiopia (which became a landlocked country following Eritrea's

49 Weldesellassie, "IGAD as an International Organization," 4.

50 Wöndu and Lesch, *Battle for Peace in Sudan*, 166–8.

51 Adar, "Conflict Resolution in a Turbulent Region," 45. See also Garang's accusations about the GoS that used the food as a weapon against the population of South Sudan: Garang and Khālid, *The Call for Democracy in Sudan*, 175–87.

52 Garang was ambiguous about that decision, fearing that it will allow GoS forces to rearm and reorganize. See: Khadiagala, *Meddlers or Mediators*, 210.

53 Adar, "Conflict Resolution in a Turbulent Region," 47.

independence)[54] collapsed several years later, when a two-year war erupted between the two states in 1998. Cliffe commented, "Granted that several countries share these problems, what can be added to their solution by tackling them at the regional as opposed to the national or community level? Or to put in slightly different terms: common problems do not necessarily or inevitably lead to regional partnership."[55]

Arguably, efforts by IGADD, and subsequently IGAD, to mediate the Sudanese conflict not only failed to achieve a resolution or even ceasefire, but even indirectly contributed to the exacerbation of the humanitarian crisis on the ground. According to Rolandsen and Daly, "...the 1990s were a dark decade for the people of South Sudan. The war claimed an unknown numbers of lives, but if casualties from indirect causes such as malnutrition and related illness are included the figure might be in the millions. Hardly any corner was spread from the fighting, and most communities suffered permanent insecurity and disruption of livelihoods."[56]

As opposed to the ambivalent, and often ineffective, nature of IGADD and IGAD mediation efforts since the mid-1980s, it seems that the new millennium carried a wind of changes with regard to IGAD's role in the Sudan mediation process. From June 2001 to January 2005, IGAD assumed an active role in various phases of the negotiations, from its initial talks to the signing of the Comprehensive Peace Agreement (CPA). It was responsible for major achievements, such a reaching agreement on the issues of self-determination, separation of state and religion, and power sharing, yet it also caused several major setbacks, as we discuss in the next chapter.

---

54 Tekle, "The Basis of Eritrean-Ethiopian Cooperation."

55 Cliffe, "Regional Dimensions of Conflict in the Horn of Africa," 104.

56 Rolandsen and Daly, *A History of South Sudan*, 132.

CHAPTER 3

We Cannot Negotiate and Fight: IGAD's Role in Achieving the CPA

Zartman's concept of "ripeness for resolution" claims that conflicts are resolvable at certain moments but not at others. In the context of extremely violent conflicts, he claims, the psycho-political dynamics requires trust-building steps before an agreement to resolve the conflict can be achieved. The "ripe" moment emerges when parties to a conflict understand that the cost of the continuing conflict is higher than the cost of entering into a negotiation process. This is opportune timing for a third party to step in. Yet, as the conflict is a process in motion, it is not always easy to recognize the moment of ripeness.[1] Did IGAD recognize the first decade of the twentieth-first century as a moment that was "ripe" for reconciliation between Sudan's South and North and therefore stepped into the position of mediator in order to exploit the opportunity?

At first glance, it seemed that the turn of the century was not the ripe moment for reconciliation. During the Eighth IGAD Summit in Khartoum in November 2000, the Heads of States noted with concern, "The slow progress in the peace negotiations between the Government of Sudan and the Sudan Peoples' Liberation Army/Movement (SPLM/A) and the continuation of the conflict in Southern Sudan that has resulted in incalculable loss of lives and destruction of property."[2] On his part, Al-Bashir "commended the efforts of President Daniel Arap Moi of Kenya in trying to bring a lasting solution to the conflict. He said that the Egyptian and Libyan initiatives should complement the efforts of IGAD, but cautioned some members of the IPF against siding with the SPLA/M."[3] At the Summit, IGAD's mediation efforts seemed to be stuck in the old limbo of mutual distrust among IGAD members that had characterized many of its previous mediation efforts; Less than a year later, global events unexpectedly changed the course of the mediation process, and the "ripe moment" for success seemed to slip away. Following the 2001 September 11 events and the US proclamation on the War on Terror, a rapprochement

1 Zartman, *Ripe for Resolution: Conflict and Intervention in Africa*.

2 IGAD, Khartoum Declaration of the Eighth Summit of Heads of State and Government, Khartoum, 27.

3 It should be mentioned that both the Egyptian and Libyan delegates to the Summit took a very cautious stand toward al-Bashir statement, claiming that their countries mediation efforts were just supplementary to those of IGAD. See: *ibid.*, 9.

 | DOI:10.1163/9789004425323_005

occurred between Sudan and the United States. In Western, and especially American, eyes, al-Bashir was considered a pro-Western moderate in comparison to al-Turabi, who was known for his pro *al-Qaeda* sympathies.[4] As a result, although Sudan remained on the list of countries sponsoring terrorism, Khartoum shared intelligence on al-Qaeda with the US, the two countries reopened diplomatic missions, and the UN lifted sanctions against Sudan. According to Khadiagala, these "high-level exchanges signaled the gradual normalization of relations."[5]

Indeed, at the turn of the century, the Horn of Africa had become identified with development of counterterrorism strategy, and during the first years of the millennium, IGAD sponsored workshops and conferences that aimed to address issues of terrorism.[6] This new interest was also related to a broader continental effort to formulate a comprehensive position on peace and security, including a clear stance toward intervention in intra-state conflicts. This effort was particularly apparent in the transition from the OAU to the AU in 2002. Compared to the former organization's ambivalent commitment to the principle of "peaceful dispute settlement," the new organization seemed to have added checks and balances and other monitoring mechanisms that were designed to make it a "more effective, democratic, and autonomous organization."[7] Moreover, on the issue of intervention in intrastate conflicts, Article 4(h) of the Constitutive Act of the AU defined "the right of the Union to intervene in a member state pursuant to a decision of the Assembly in respect of grave circumstances, namely war crimes, genocide and crimes against humanity."[8] Another mechanism established to prevent, control, and resolve African conflicts was the Peace and Security Council (PSC). Comprising 15 rotating members, the PSC was established to coordinate all responses to events involving grave human rights violations. New mechanisms for improving coordination between the various AU organs and the regional organizations were also developed,[9] and one of the most important of these was the Conflict Early Warning and Response Mechanism (CEWRAN). Faced with the complex challenges of ongoing conflicts, AU members recognized the significance of preventive action prior

4 Al-Qaeda leader, Osama Bin-Laden, had made a home in Sudan from 1991 to 1996, a period where al-Turabi was still an influential political figure in the revolutionary regime.

5 Khadiagala, *Meddlers or Mediators? African Interveners in Civil Conflicts in Eastern Africa*, 239.

6 See, for example: Report on IGAD Conference on the Prevention and Combating of Terrorism UN Conference Centre.

7 Zweifel, *International Organizations and Democracy: Accountability, Politics, and Power*, 148.

8 African Union, Constitutive Act of the African Union, Article 4(h), July 11, 2000.

9 For a detailed analysis of this issue, see: Abedajo, "The Peacekeeping Travails of the AU and the Regional Economic Communities."

to their escalation. The decision to create an early warning and response mechanism had already been adopted at a summit in April 1998; In September 2002, members decided that the mechanism would cover four main areas: pastoral communities and cattle rustling, small arms and environmental security, the peace process, and civil society.[10]

In 2002, IGAD was the first regional organization to operate such a mechanism, which, in general, reflected the belief that gathering information in the early stages of escalating crises and analyzing the possible responses to them could contribute to conflict prevention.[11] CEWRAN included local people as stakeholders in the process; collaboration between civil society and governments; and cooperation between regional, continental and international organizations.[12] The positive and negative effects of CEWARN on IGAD's mediation efforts in South Sudan are discussed later.

As a result of the rapprochement between the West and the GoS, the latter agreed to accept IGAD's renewed mediation efforts.[13] The United States appointed former Senator John Danforth as the Bush administration's special envoy to Sudan. Initially, Danforth's goals were limited, and he was instructed to focus on securing a temporary ceasefire, facilitating the delivery of humanitarian aid, and improving the humanitarian situation in the Nuba Mountains. It also seemed that Danforth's position on how to approach the rivals was far removed from IGAD's own ideas, especially on the core issues of separation of state and religion and self-determination of the South. Danforth believed that "Sudan would not become a secular state, and self-determination would not encompass independence for the South."[14] In a special report to the president of the United States, he contended,

> The view that self-determination includes the guaranteed option of secession is contained in the IGAD Declaration of Principles, and is supported by many Sudanese. However, secession would be strongly resisted by the Government of Sudan, and would be exceedingly difficult to achieve. A more feasible, and, I think, preferable view of self-determination would ensure the right of the people of southern Sudan to live under a government that respects their religion and culture. Such a system would require

10 Juma, "The Intergovernmental Authority on Development and the East African Community," 239–41.

11 Christensen, "Conflict Early Warning and Response Mechanism in the Horn of Africa."

12 Weldesellassie, "IGAD as an International Organization, Its Institutional Development and Shortcomings," 12–3.

13 Young, "Sudan IGAD Peace Process; An Evaluation," 13–4.

14 Johnson, *The Root Causes of Sudan's Civil Wars*, 178.

> robust internal and external guarantees so that any promises made by the Government in peace negotiations could not be ignored in practice.[15]

Over time, however, Danforth adopted an approach much closer to that of IGAD and the IPF, and combined forces with them to reinvigorate the negotiation process.[16] This meeting of minds was the starting point of almost three years of intense mediation efforts that eventually led to the signing of the CPA. Before describing the nature and developments of the negotiation process, and IGAD's role there, a brief description of the rival parties' motivations to rejoin the negotiation table is required.

The GoS's motives to return to the negotiation table were, in part, related to its deteriorating military position in the South. Since 1998, the prospects of a Northern military victory diminished after the two longstanding Southern rivals, John Garang and Riek Machar, resolved their differences and merged the two largest rival factions in 2002, shattering Northern hopes that internal divisions in the South would preclude a unified front.[17]

Adding to the political unification and increasing military power in the South was the economic cost of the war, which itself was related to Sudan's oil economy. During the 1990s and the first years of the twenty-first century, Sudan experienced an "oil boom."[18] As access to the new oil fields became blocked by SPLM/A attacks, the GoS grasped that the potential income loss, combined with the enormous cost of the war itself, required a renewed commitment to resolve the conflict with the South.[19]

This understanding of the need to resolve the conflict was not related solely to the GoS's relations with the South. Another, probably major consideration in the GoS's eagerness to reach an agreement with the South was the deteriorating situation in Sudan's western region, Darfur. Although the severe humanitarian crisis in this region came to international attention as early as 2003,

15 Danforth, *Report to the President of the United States on the Outlook for Peace in Sudan*, 24–5.

16 Khadiagala, *Meddlers or Mediators?* 239–40.

17 It is important to note, however, that the rapprochement between Garang and Machar was also a response to heavy pressure by the Americans. See: Natsios. *Sudan, South Sudan, and Darfur*, 163–4.

18 Increasing interest in Sudanese oil by Asian countries (and particularly China) spurred the country's GDP growth from 2.9 percent between 1980 and 1998, to an average of 7.9 percent between 2004 and 2008. See: Patey, "Crude Days Ahead? Oil and the Resource Curse in Sudan," 619–20.

19 Despite the growing revenues from the oil production, the GoS suffered from a constant state of economic instability, See: *ibid.*

international acknowledgment about the situation in Darfur was slow to develop. Gérard Prunier claimed that international hopes for ending one of the longest, most brutal civil wars in post-colonial Africa eclipsed international action on Darfur. These hopes created a "feel good factor" that helped the Sudanese government deny the initial rumors about an armed conflict developing in its western region.[20] However, one of the crucial challenges left unresolved in the CPA was the issue of internal borders and the cohesion of the two political entities that were created following dissolution. Sudan had to face the risk that dissolution would weaken its political center and have a destabilizing effect on other provinces, such as Darfur, Southern Kordofan, and the Blue Nile. As noted, since the beginning of the negotiations over the CPA, the Government of Sudan responded violently to the conflict percolating in its western province. As discussed later, the effect of the events in Darfur on the negotiation process between the North and the South were more significant than they first seemed.

In the case of North-South conflict, which was portrayed as a predominantly religious-based dispute, it was more difficult to justify the use of violence against the inhabitants of Darfur, who are predominantly Muslims. In this context, Gérard Prunier claimed, "The North-South conflict has been in many of its aspects a colonial conflict, while the Darfur uprising was from the beginning much closer to a genuine civil war. And civil wars are often the most relentless forms of conflict because they involve relatives. In Khartoum, the government panicked because it suddenly felt that the Muslim family was splintering, potentially with enormous consequences."[21] Khartoum appeared to be determined to maintain the cohesion of the "remainder" of the country, even at the cost of its declining international status. From the perspective of the peripheries, South Sudan's success to determine its own fate motivated various secessionists' demands, including the demands raised by several (but not all) groups in Darfur.[22]

The SPLM/A had its own reasons to return to the negotiating table. Their newly achieved internal unity, military successes, and massive international support for their cause, which was soaring at the time, made this a "ripe moment" for investing efforts to achieve their goals in issues such as power sharing and wealth sharing.[23] The emerging oil industry led to a dual understanding:

20 Prunier, *Darfur: The Ambiguous Genocide*, 88–91.

21 *Ibid.*, XI.

22 Medani, "Strife and Secession in Sudan."

23 Ylönen, however, claimed that the rapprochement between Washington and Khartoum threatened SPLM/A's traditional position the "favorite" of the American administration

fear that oil revenues would strengthen the power of the Northern government (indeed, some people argued that the GoS merely joined the talks as a delay tactic to gain full control of the oil fields), alongside the desire to secure a share of the oil revenues. Despite the strong motives of both parties, it soon became clear that many obstacles lay in the negotiators' long path to an agreement, and even more so, until its implementation.

There is broad agreement among scholars that the Machakos talks of June-July 2002 – and specifically the unexpected willingness of the Sudanese government to accept the IGAD Declaration of Principles (DoP) as the basis for the renewed negotiations – marked the turning point in the negotiation process between the South and the North. Scholars also concur that, notwithstanding the active American involvement and the help of the British, Norwegians, Italians, Swiss, and others as facilitators in the negotiations,[24] it was IGAD's involvement that made the breakthrough in the negotiation process possible,[25] and specifically the personal commitment of Kenyan President Daniel Arap Moi, and his November 2001 decision to appoint Lieutenant General Lazaro Sumbeiywo as special envoy to the IGAD Peace Process on Sudan. According to John Young, Sumbeiywo was "the grand facilitator and moral guarantor, maintaining the respect for the process, keeping thing together and stepping in at key moments."[26] Sumbeiywo's official biographer offers some insights into Moi's choice of Sumbeiywo, and analyzes the mediation skills and abilities that contributed to his success:

> Why had Moi decided on Sumbeiywo? First, the army officer was well versed with the conflicts of the region, as Director of the Military Intelligence and later as the head of the Liaison Department, he had immense intelligence on what was happening beyond Kenya's border. Secondly, Moi needed someone he could trust. He was closed to Sumbeiywo and knew the man had an independent spirit ... Thirdly, the combatants in the conflict were all military people. President Omar Bashir was a military officer who had overthrown a civilian government and John Garang was a hardened guerilla leader who had led the life of a military General. The task at hand will be better handled by someone who understood the

---

and public. See: Ylönen, "Security Regionalism and Flaws of Externally Forged Peace in Sudan: The IGAD Peace Process and its Aftermath," 27.

24 See, for example, an analysis of the Swiss involvement in the mediation process: Mason, "Learning from the Swiss Mediation and Facilitation Experiences in Sudan."

25 See, for example: Johnson, *The Root Causes of Sudan's Civil Wars,* 179–80; Rolandsen and Daly, *A History of South Sudan: From Slavery to Independence,* 135–7; Khadiagala, *Meddlers or Mediators,* 239–43.

26 Young, "Sudan IGAD Peace Process," 18.

> mind of a military general rather than a diplomat who might be bogged down with the necessities of diplomatese. Moi's involvement with Sudan was so passionate that he wanted a man who would translate his desires into actions.[27]

Sumbeiywo did not hesitate to bring into the process foreign experts such as Susan Page, an American diplomat, Nicholas Haysom, a South African constitutional lawyer, and Julian Hottinger of the Swiss Federal Department of Foreign Affairs, to work alongside the IPF observer team. Added to these experts was a team of three IGAD envoys from Eritrea, Ethiopia, and Uganda. He also did not hesitate to use the good advice of well-known figures, including former US President Jimmy Carter:

> The negotiations took a very interesting turn at Machakos. For 29 days the two sides were mostly shouting at each other. But while they were shouting I was making notes on the issues. After 29 days we prepared a text. President Carter had advised me that without a single negotiating text I risked losing the process. So I translated the DoP into a single text and then zeroed in on the two main issues: self-determination and the separation of state and religion. Wealth sharing, security, power sharing, the judiciary, civil rights and so forth were also in the framework.[28]

Indeed, the Machakos Protocol mentioned this unequivocally:

> That the people of South Sudan have the right to self-determination, inter alia, through a referendum to determine their future status. At the end of the six (6) year interim period there shall be an internationally monitored referendum, organized jointly by the GOS and the SPLM/A, for the people of South Sudan to: confirm the unity of the Sudan by voting to adopt the system of government established under the Peace Agreement; or to vote for secession.[29]

Another fundamental issue that was addressed at the negotiating table was related to the length of the interim period and the date of the referendum: The GoS that insisted that the referendum would be held in ten years, and the

27 Waihenya. *The Mediator. Gen. Lazaro Sumbeiywo and the Southern Sudan Peace Process*, 38–9.

28 IGAD, "The Mediator's Perspective; An Interview with General Lazaro Sumbeiywo."

29 Agreed text on the Right for Self-Determination for the People of South Sudan. The Machakos Protocol (or Chapter I), signed in Machakos, Kenya on July 20, 2002.

SPLM/A demanded a wait of no more than two years; the compromise was that the referendum would be held within six years.[30] Kumar Rupesinghe emphasizes the importance of defining a timetable that is not too long nor too short: If the timetable is too long and the negotiations continue for a long time, the drive for peace may dissipate. If the duration is too short, there is a risk of sufficient trust and the process fails to develop.

The next breakthrough occurred in a meeting between Garang and al-Bashir held in Kampala under the auspicious of IGAD, soon after the signing of the Machakos Protocol. At this meeting, the first one-on-one meeting of the two leaders, they declared their commitment to the peace process and to achieving a comprehensive political settlement.[31] The optimism that colored the joint meeting of the parties' leaders and the protocol they signed was soon overshadowed by the GoS's retreat from some sections of the protocol (including insistence to replace "independence" and "secession" with the phrase "making unity attractive") and by events on ground. The SPLM/A's capture of the small town of Torit in September 2002 was a major setback to the efforts to build trust between the parties. The capture of this city was particularly painful for the GoS, as casualties included Mulla Ahmed Haj Nur, a close friend of Bashir, and other high-ranking Northern officers.[32] When, in response to the incident in Torit, the parties were instructed to cease all fighting during the talks, the qualities of IGAD's mediation skills were revealed. When Sumbeiywo complained to President Moi, "These people do not understand anything other than a barrel of gun," Moi replied, "*We cannot negotiate and fight. Let's go back to the negotiating table.*" (emphasis added)[33] One month later, after IGAD mediated this critical phase in the negotiations, both parties signed the Memorandum of Understanding and Cessation of Hostilities,[34] agreeing to resume the talks immediately. This stage in the talks reveals several important features of IGAD's mode of mediation. The first feature was Moi's commitment to the process. In general, Kenyan dominance in the negotiation process was attributed mostly to President Moi. When Moi's party KANU lost the 2002 elections and Mwai Kibaki replaced him as the president of Kenya, deep concerns arose regarding the fate of the negotiation process as a result of the absence of Moi's

30 *Ibid.*, 87.

31 Khadiagala, *Meddlers or Mediators*, 242.

32 Young, "Sudan IGAD Peace Process," 18.

33 Waihenya, *The Mediator. Gen. Lazaro Sumbeiywo*, 97.

34 A more effective agreement, signed in Karen on February 4, 2003, led to the creation of the Verification Monitoring Team (VMT) that reported directly to the special envoy.

commitment and passion.[35] In effect, the lesser commitment of Moi's successor to the IGAD mediation process hampered progress in the negotiations.

The second feature was IGAD's responsiveness to the demand for an inclusive mediation process. To perform its role as mediator, IGAD relied on politicians and diplomats, but also on civilians and civil-society groups. In fact, IGAD's commitment to integrate the people's voices was not limited to its conflict resolution efforts. The establishment of an organ such as the IGAD Women's Desk highlighted the importance of listening to women's voices in a region where women's political and diplomatic participation is low and they face enormous problems as result of natural and human-made disasters.[36] To tackle this issue, IGAD conducted seminars on core issues, such as wealth-sharing and political-sharing, which included both experts and representatives of different segments of society. Khadiagala believed that "by sounding out different voices, the mediators also hoped to make the negotiations more participatory."[37] Moreover, when the talks reached a deadlock during the second half of 2003, Sumbeiywo and the IGAD Secretariat decided to travel to many parts of South and North Sudan to hear the voices of the people and develop a more holistic understanding of the parties involved in the process, as he described:

> I went to Sudan and met many people: civil society, religious groups, lawyers, judges, everybody. Having retired from the Kenyan army at the end of February 2003, I had time to travel. I went with the Machakos framework and tried to find out the positions of the parties regarding all the issues, the issues of security, power sharing, wealth sharing.[38]

The third feature was IGAD's attention to the conflict's psycho-historical roots and its desire to help the parties work through their country's "bad history" of marginalization, slavery, and other bad memories. IGAD-organized workshops and plenary sessions explored questions such as "What does it mean to be African?," "What does slavery mean to you?" and "What does self-determination mean to you?."[39] Rupesinghe underlines the importance of a clear conceptual and theoretical understanding of the root causes and sources of intractability of a conflict. Therefore, it is imperative that conflict resolution facilitators

35 Waihenya, *The Mediator. Gen. Lazaro Sumbeiywo*, 100–1.
36 Weldesellassie, "IGAD as an International Organization," 11–12.
37 Khadiagala, *Meddlers or Mediators*, 242.
38 IGAD, "The Mediator's Perspective; An Interview with General Lazaro Sumbeiywo," 24.
39 Waihenya, *The Mediator. Gen. Lazaro Sumbeiywo*, 86–7.

come to grips with how and why a conflict erupted so that the sources, which generated the conflict, can be addressed.[40]

IGAD policy-makers' recognition of the importance of integrating less conventional aspects into the mediation process, such as emotions and memories, rather than focusing solely on the more formal elements of diplomacy, might have served as an important tool to further the processes of its mediation efforts. Unfortunately, the CPA that was eventually signed showed ultimately all the parties including IGAD abandoned their commitment to include various segments of the Sudanese and South Sudanese societies in the final stages of the negotiation process.

The next phase of the talks took place in Nakuru, Kenya, in July 2003. After months with no progress, the IGAD mediation team proposed the Nakuru Framework, a document that aimed to resolve the issues that had remained unresolved from the Machakos Protocol, which was effectively rejected by the GoS.[41] GoS negotiators even applied to South Africa, during an AU meeting in Maputo, to mediate in the peace process instead of IGAD, but their initiative was swiftly blocked by IGAD representatives at Maputo.[42] The next phase of the negotiations was held in Naivasha, Kenya, and it was this phase that eventually led to signing the CPA. Yet, before proceeding to an account of Naivasha talks, it is important to briefly mention one of the major setbacks of the negotiation process that had already come to light during the Nakuru talks of 2003: The Sudanese conflict was inseparably linked to the fate of Sudan's other regions.

This understanding was a fundamental component of John Garang's worldview. Already in the 1980s, he cautioned:

> It is often forgotten that the Sudan is not just north and south. The Sudan is also west, east, and center, no matter what definitions you wish to attach to these labels... All patriots must appreciate the reality that we are a new breed of Sudanese; we will not accept being fossilized into subcitizens in the 'Regions.'[43]

---

40 Rupesinghe, *Conflict Transformation*, 166.

41 They were rejected both by al-Bashir (who reportedly told the IGAD team mediation to "go to hell"), and GoS negotiating team member Muhamad Dirdeiry (who is quoted as saying, "The only way out is to throw out the IGAD document"). See: Waihenya, *The Mediator. Gen. Lazaro Sumbeiywo*, 86–7.

42 Kwaje,"The Sudan Peace Process, From Machakos to Naivasha"; Young, "Sudan IGAD Peace Process," 18.

43 Garang, *John Garang Speaks*, 93.

Garang's vision for a "New Sudan" entailed a new division of political power in a united state, reflecting the equal status of all Sudanese as stakeholders, irrespective of race, ethnic affiliation, gender, or other factors. The alternative, he stated, was to divide the country.[44] The areas of the Blue Nile and Southern Kordofan (where the Nuba Mountains are located) had a long history of marginalization and had been a target of land grabbing for commercial use, exploitation of natural resources, such as minerals, and the Blue Nile River, since Sudan's independence. As a result, underdevelopment of the state was a continuous source of tension between the local population and the government in Khartoum, and was one of the reasons that Blue Nile inhabitants joined the SPLM during Sudan's second civil war. Moreover, about quarter of the SPLA soldiers were from the Nuba Mountain. The Blue Nile State was an important theatre of the second Sudanese civil war, and the SPLM enjoyed the support of many of the local Funj (the "indigenous" African communities of Blue Nile).[45]

Loyal to his vision of a "New Sudan," Garang insisted on integrating the issue of the "other regions" into a comprehensive solution, Indeed, these issues had become part of the negotiations process between the South and the North already during Nairobi talks in 1998. The SPLM/A insisted that Southern Kordofan, Southern Blue Nile, and the Abyei, an area mostly inhabited by the Dinka that had been annexed to North Sudan by the British in 1956, would be defined as part of the South. The GoS, in contrast, insisted that the boundaries that existed at independence (which defined the South as the States of Bahr al-Ghazal, Equatoria, and Upper Nile) should be the basis for further negotiations.[46]

The issue of the "contested regions" (the Blue Nile, Southern Kordofan, and Abyei) repeatedly threatened to undermine the peace process. As the problems of the contested areas were not included in the Machakos protocol, protocol critics frequently accused the SPLM/A of betraying the interests of these regions in the protocol for the sake of its own interests. The GoS argued that the three contested areas were north of the 1956 boundary and therefore outside IGAD's mandate. Later, when the parties resumed talks in Karen, Eritrea, in January 2003, it seemed that the same grievances of the Southern people concerning exclusion and marginalization were mirrored in the grievances of the people of the contested regions. The representatives of Southern Blue Nile, for example, protested against the GoS's declaration of *jihad* against the Funj people, which included forced Arabization and Islamization, and

44 Gibia, *John Garang and the Vision of New Sudan*.
45 Adar, "Conflict Resolution in a Turbulent Region," 51–2.
46 Khadiagala, *Meddlers or Mediators*, 211.

religious persecution. The Ngok Dinka of the Abyei region, who asserted a connection to the Dinka in the South, demanded equal rights of self-determination. The Nuba Mountains delegation also insisted on self-determination, and the Southern Kordofan asked for equal rights in the process. The roles of IGAD's mediation team, led by Sumbeiywo, become increasingly difficult and frustrating.[47]

Despite the importance of the fates of Southern Blue Nile, the Southern Kordofan, and Abyei, which is discussed in greater detail below, the events that would have the most powerful impact on North-South negotiations for peace occurred in Darfur, where a large-scale civil war raged. The situation in Darfur had escalated since the 1990s "from resource-based conflicts to crimes against humanity,"[48] mainly due to Darfur's ongoing marginalization and acute deprivation, and the increasingly violent battle over resources, combined with assimilation of racist terminology. Since the first attack by local groups that targeted the small town of Golu on February 26, 2003, and resulted in the deaths of 200 Sudanese army soldiers, clashes between the GoS and the two local Darfurian groups – the Sudan Liberation Army (SLA) and the Justice and Equality Movement (JEM) – persisted with growing frequency. The local forces scored victories in additional parts of Darfur later that year, including the conquest of al-Fasher airport and the city of Kotum in April. The GoS was quick to respond, both directly, in the form of air raids on Darfurian villages, and indirectly, by activating the quasi-governmental *Janjaweed* militias. As a pre-emptive strike to deter rebel mobilization among the Darfur tribes, the GoS launched a security crackdown on the *Fur*, *Massalit*, and *Zaghawa* populations. Educated young men and people related to the rebels by kinship or residence were detained, intimidated, tortured, and in some cases killed. In 2004, the gravity of the situation led US Secretary of State Colin Powell to define the events in Darfur as genocide:

> "We concluded that genocide has been committed in Darfur and that the government of Sudan and the Janjaweed bear responsibility and genocide may still be occurring," he declared in September of that year. The testimonies gathered in the camps [refugees' camps in Chad], he said, showed a pattern of violence which was coordinated, not random.[49]

47 Waihenya, *The Mediator. Gen. Lazaro Sumbeiywo and the Southern Sudan Peace Process*, 109–10.

48 Iyob and Khadiagala, *Sudan: The Elusive Quest for Peace*, 101–32.

49 "Powell Declares Genocide in Sudan."

One possible explanation for the severity of the GoS's response to the insurgence in Darfur was its concern that the escalating situation would affect the peace process with the South, which at the time was regarded as a main source of Khartoum's legitimacy in the international arena. The GoS adamantly objected to the inclusion of Darfur in the negotiations. When SPLM/A leader John Garang expressed explicit interest in extending the North-South peace process to include Darfur, and proposed a deployment of 10,000 SPLA troops in Darfur as part of the AU peacekeeping force,[50] the GoS quickly rejected his proposal.

In a review of IGAD's motives to mediate a resolution of the conflict between the North and the South, it is important to clarify that the reason for IGAD's noninvolvement in Darfur was the fact that the case of Darfur was already "being taken care of" by other regional organizations. In fact, the African Union's decision to deploy AMIS (African Union Mission in Sudan), an observers' mission that later become a multi-functional hybrid force of the UN and the AU (known as UNAMID), was considered a precedent that changed the discourse about sovereignty and intervention in intrastate conflicts.[51] Yet, the desire to avoid overlap with the continental organization cannot fully explain IGAD's objections to Darfur's inclusion in the negotiations: since AMIS was not meant to be a mediator force, IGAD could be considered as a complementary mediation force to promote dialogue between the rival parties.

IGAD's limited interest to implement its mediation efforts in Darfur might also be explained by the fact that the various actors in the international community, which wished to conclude the peace negotiations between the South and the North, put pressure on IGAD not to intervene. According to Barltrop, in 2003, the Troika, comprising the United States, Britain, and Norway, together with other IGAD partners, encouraged IGAD to focus on the CPA and ignore the case of Darfur.[52] It became more difficult to defend this position in 2004, when the situation on the ground in Darfur was deteriorating rapidly,[53] and international public awareness of the crisis increased. Yet, the fear of jeopardizing the IGAD talks between the North and the South prevented the Troika from

---

50 Mulama, "Darfur Overshadows the Peace Process in South Sudan."

51 For a comprehensive discussion in this issue, see: Back, *Intervention and Sovereignty in Africa*, 37–8, 42.

52 Barltrop, *Darfur and the International Community: The Challenges of Conflict Resolution in Sudan*.

53 Mulama claims that: "Aid agencies say up to 50,000 people have died from the conflict, while more than 1.4 million have been displaced internally. About 170,000 of these have fled into neighboring Chad for fear of being attacked by the Janjaweed." See: Mulama, "Darfur Overshadows the Peace Process in South Sudan."

advocating intervention in the case of Darfur. Instead, "the Troika began to argue publicly that IGAD peace process will benefit Darfur by providing a 'template' agreement for resolving the Darfur conflict."[54]

Indeed, IGAD's focused efforts in the North-South negotiations led to another breakthrough in Naivasha. In contrast to the Machakos talks, which involved mid-level delegations, the Naivasha talks marked a long-awaited turning point in the course of the negotiations, triggered by the transition from two-party dominance to the dominance of two persons on the team negotiating on behalf of the South: SPLM/A leader John Garang and Ali Osamn Taha, first vice president of Sudan at the time. This transition was threatened by last-minute events, and particularly the late arrival of Garang to the meeting, as Sumbeiywo recalled:

> I called the Kenyan Minister of Foreign Affairs, Stephen Musyoka, in Cairo and asked him to see President al-Bashir in Khartoum and ask for his vice-president to come and negotiate with Dr John Garang. Garang agreed to come to Naivasha on 1 September. Al-Bashir was reluctant, saying John Garang had twice snubbed his vice-president, and a third time would be really catastrophic. But eventually we agreed on a four-day meeting from 1 September – hoping that it was going to be very short. For three days Garang didn't come! This was very difficult! His officers were insisting that he should only negotiate with the president himself. Two SPLM people helped me: Dr Justin Yaac Arop and Commander Deng Alor, who were in Nairobi. John Garang wrote a letter to Musyoka saying they would reschedule the meeting. Dr Justin gets the letter, puts it in his pocket, but doesn't give it to Musyoka. He puts pressure on Garang by writing to him that he should not dream of going back to Kenya, because the Kenyans were mad at him! They would not want to see him and his family would be kicked out. On the third day at 6 o'clock John Garang arrives in Naivasha! By 6:30 we had put Ali Osman Taha and Garang together, the first time they had met face to face. They asked us to leave them alone to talk, to get to know each other.[55]

Despite the rough starting point, IGAD's diplomatic experience, and especially Sumbeiywo's patience, created a point of no return in the negotiations, which led to the signing of an agreement on security issues on September 25, 2003:

---

54 Barltrop, *Darfur and the International Community*, 127.

55 IGAD, "The Mediator's Perspective; An Interview with General Lazaro Sumbeiywo," 24–5. See also Waihenya, *The Mediator*, 122–3.

"Over a three-month period, talks between Taha and Garang changed the negotiations' atmosphere and pace, deepened the chemistry between the two leaders, and boosted the parties' ownership of the peace process."[56] The parties continued to discuss issues of wealth and power sharing, as well the fate of the contested Three Areas for the next several months, and it seemed likely that a comprehensive peace agreement would be signed by the end of that year. However, the dynamic of the negotiation process, and particularly the changed "chemistry between the two leaders"[57] postponed the conclusion of the process by several months.

The Naivasha talks were finally concluded in January 2005, with the signing of the parties on the Comprehensive Peace Agreement (CPA). The days before the signing of the agreement were tense: Even the formal ceremony was preceded by a series of last-minutes crises.[58] Still, the signing event could be considered a triumph for regional mediation efforts, and in particular for IGAD, which was lauded by Uganda. In his speech at the ceremony, President Yuwery Museveni stated, "We in the IGAD region and Africa as a whole have created a viable partnership, which reduces chances for outsiders to jump into solving regional conflicts yet they have very little knowledge about them."[59]

Although Museneni may have unfairly discounted the contribution of international diplomatic and financial support that was undoubtedly critical to the success of the process, in many respects the CPA could be considered the continuation of previous agreements brokered by regional mediation efforts, extending from the 1972 Addis Ababa agreement to the Machakos Protocol of 2002. The CPA was based on IGAD's previous frameworks of solution to the Sudanese conflict and the wording of the DOP. The first paragraph of the CPA stressed IGAD's role in the process:

> WHEREAS the Government of the Republic of the Sudan (GOS) and the Sudan People's Liberation Movement/Sudan People's Liberation Army (SPLM/A) (hereinafter referred to as the "Parties"), having met in continuous negotiations between May 2002 and December 2004, in Karen, Machakos, Nairobi, Nakuru, Nanyuki and Naivasha, Kenya, under the auspices of the Inter-Governmental Authority on Development (IGAD) Peace Process ... and, in respect of the issues related to the Conflict Areas

56 Khadiagala, *Meddlers or Mediators*, 243.
57 *Ibid.*
58 For a detailed description, see Waihenya, *The Mediator*, 139–43.
59 Quoted in Khadiagala, *Meddlers or Mediators*, 246.

> of Southern Kordofan and Blue Nile States and Abyei Area, under the auspices of the Government of the Republic of Kenya.[60]

The CPA appeared to be a solid achievement, but a careful reading of the 260-page CPA reveals several potential obstacles to its implementation, mainly in the form of unresolved issues. First, the contested areas were mentioned in the opening paragraph of the CPA, and addressed in two separate chapters, yet many issues were inadequately resolved. The first chapter addressed the fate of South Kordofan, Nuba Mountains, and Blue Nile areas at length[61] and noted that the decision to join to the South or the North would be made by "popular consultations," yet these areas were not included within the future borders of South Sudan. The second chapter focused on the resource-rich Abyei region.[62] In effect, breaking the deadlock surrounding this region allowed the parties to move to the final stage of signing the CPA. According to the CPA, simultaneously with the referendum for southern Sudan, the residents of Abyei would cast a separate ballot on whether the region would retain its special administrative status in the north or would become part of Bahr el Ghazal.[63] Demarcation of the borders in the Abyei region was also left unresolved. The ambiguous status of Abyei ignited the conflict between the South and the North immediately after independence.[64]

Second, the CPA was not a truly inclusive document. Despite IGAD's efforts to create an inclusive dialogue that includes a variety of Southern and Northern voices, the final stage of the negotiating process was rather exclusive and elitist in its nature, including mostly the representatives of the GoS and the SPLM/A. On the issue of the inclusiveness of the final stages of the CPA negotiations, John Young states that both parties integrated civil society and non-governmental groups merely for the sake of appearance:

> In the final stages of the negotiations the mediators, the GoS, and the SPLM/A became increasingly aware that to achieve acceptance and gain legitimacy the peace settlement needed the support of the Sudanese public. As a result, the SPLM/A began to respond to demands of southern civil society, one of which was a strong commitment to self-determination,

60 African Union, Comprehensive Peace Agreement between the Government of the Republic of Sudan and the Sudan People Liberation Movement/Army, xi.

61 *Ibid.*, 71–84.

62 *Ibid.*, 63–70.

63 *Ibid.*, 65–6.

64 Ylönen, "The Sudan-South Sudan Military Escalation in Heglig: Shifting Attention from Domestic Challenges."

> and attempt to allay the fears of the NDA that its interests were not being considered in the negotiations. The GoS in turn took various non-governmental groups, including members from the leading opposition parties, civil society groups, nationally known figures, tribal leaders, and even Sufis to Naivasha. However, their role was limited to providing legitimacy for an agreement that had almost been finalised, and as one member of the GoS admitted, "It was largely an exercise in public relations."[65]

Despite the SPLM/A's relatively inclusive mode of negotiations, the movement quickly reverted to its authoritarian and elitist nature were after the signing of the agreement.

Following the final agreement, the parties agreed on an interim period of six years, to be followed by a referendum. Under the referendum, South Sudanese would choose between independence or uniting with the North under the system of government established under the peace agreement. Yet, both the mediators and the negotiating parties paid little attention to the mechanisms for managing the interim period. Indeed, many of the major problems of the future South Sudanese state, such as authoritarianism, leadership splits, ethnic rivalry, and other evils, emerged during the interim period, and no checks and balances were in place to curtail them. The following chapter traces IGAD's role in the major developments of this important six-year transition period up to the referendum and the first two years after independence.

65 Young, "Sudan IGAD Peace Process," 23.

CHAPTER 4

Spring of Hope? IGAD's Mediation Efforts 2005–2014

As the parties prepared for the six-year transition period after signing the CPA in 2005, a dramatic event occurred that changed the course of events in Sudan. Even prior to the final signing of the CPA, John Garang had expressed his discomfort with the emerging agreement. Speaking to the Voice of America on May 30, 2004, he said, "This peace agreement was reached, not necessarily because the parties wanted to, but because both parties were forced to … by a set of pressures. The cost of continuing the war was felt by both sides to be much higher than the cost of stopping the war. So, we stopped the war."[1] Splitting the Sudanese state into North and South largely contradicted his "New Sudan" vision, and it is reasonable to assume that he would have liked to promote his agenda as Sudan's first vice president, a position for which he was nominated after the CPA was signed. Yet, similar to the tragedy of Moses who saw the Promised Land but would never enter it, John Garang died in a helicopter crash on July 30, 2005, only several weeks after his nomination. His death, which many believed was the result of a successful assassination attempt, ignited a wave of riots and violence in the capital Khartoum and other towns. The riots and the fact that many of the protestors were from Darfur and the Nuba Mountains confirmed Khartoum's fears that the south's secession would have a domino effect on other restive provinces such as Darfur, Kordofan, and the Blue Nile, over which the government was determined to retain sovereign control.[2]

These suspicions were also fed by the SPLM/A's new leadership: Salva Kiir Mayardyt, Garang's former deputy and his successor following his death, was identified with a much more actively secessionist position than his predecessor.[3] During the remainder of the interim period, Kiir advocated a clear-cut policy of succession, diminishing hopes that the South would choose unity over independence. This change in the South's position heightened the tensions between the leaders of the South and the North, which prompted IGAD's return to its mediating role in Sudan.

1 Justice Africa, "Prospects for Peace in Sudan."
2 Young, "John Garang's Legacy to the Peace Process, the SPLM/A & the South."
3 Ylönen, "Security Regionalism and Flaws of Externally Forged Peace in Sudan," 30.

 | DOI:10.1163/9789004425323_006

The signing of the CPA in 2005 had raised hopes that the dark clouds of the devastating decades-long civil war between the North and the South in Sudan were finally dissipating. The detailed agreement covered many crucial topics such as wealth sharing and political power sharing, future democratization, and even possible independence for the South after the interim period of six years, according to the results of a referendum that was supposed to be held in 2011.[4] When the CPA was signed, it therefore appeared that there would be little need for IGAD's mediation efforts in the future. Although IGAD was required to step back to the mediation arena sooner than was expected to address new developments that occurred both inside the North and the South, as well as between them, the period from 2005 to late 2013 (from the signing on the CPA to the end of the first two years of independence) demanded more limited mediation efforts by IGAD. Focusing on IGAD's renewed mediation efforts in this period, this chapter shows how the parties missed many opportunities to create a stable peace.

Already during in the transition period between the signing of the CPA and South Sudan's independence, it turned out that, to paraphrase Hamlet, "Something was rotten" in the State of South Sudan, and problems surfaced at a rapid pace. It initially seemed that Garang's tragic death would not crush the hopes planted by the CPA, and that Salva Kiir Mayardit would be able to fill his legendary predecessor's place and handle the implementation of the agreement effectively, yet political struggles, ideological splits, and economic mismanagement quickly emerged as obstacles.

Political tensions soon came to light between Salva Kiir, a veteran guerilla from the first civil war, who was Garang's deputy and one of the founding members of the SPLM/A, and Riek Machar Teny, also a veteran and a third-ranking member of the SPLM/A. The rivalry between the two political figures was related to their ethnic affiliations and to their ideological inclinations. Kiir was from the Dinka and Machar from the Nuer, the two main ethnic groups that had been competing over political, military, and economic dominance since the second civil war.[5] In addition, Kiir promoted the idea of South Sudan's independence, while Machar, a traditional ally of Khartoum, defended Garang's vision of "New Sudan." As the idea of Southern succession was much more popular among the people of the South, Kiir was able to create a semblance of national unity, all the while appointing his close associates to positions in political and military

4 *Africa News*, "Sudan; AU Commission Chairman Urges Country to Rise to Referendum Challenge in 2011."

5 For a detailed discussion in the roots of this rivalry, see: Jok and Hutchinson, "Sudan's Prolonged Second Civil War and the Militarization of Nuer and Dinka Ethnic Identities."

offices.[6] These political and ideological rivalries persisted and were accompanied by the general debilitation of the political institutions of the coming-into-being state, described in a special report by the Juba-based Sudd Institute:

> One unfortunate, not so clever way of conducting public affairs that the ruling elites have embraced since the signing of CPA has been a "single task" approach whereby many pressing issues were literally swept under the carpet with the aim of being addressed later. This attitude is best shown by how the entirety of the interim period was approached, downplaying the importance of reconciliation processes in ensuring healthy transition. Instead of the SPLM working to translate some of its wartime rhetoric into reality so as to cement the gains made, the common preoccupation of the political leadership during the said period was to ensure that referendum took place in order to settle the questions of unity or separation once and for all. The view shown towards the gathering mountains of challenges by those tasked with guiding the state was usually that these issues will be settled later, intimating an apparent lack of ability to multitask in a very high-paced environment. Sadly, the expected gains seemed to have never materialized, but the realities that have been perennially avoided have now gone burst with damming consequences. The other preoccupation by the SPLM elite has been corruption, which has nearly bankrupted the infant nation.[7]

From an economic perspective, Patey argues that the CPA negotiation period and the interim phase were a missed opportunity to support the development efforts in southern Sudan. The wealth-sharing provisions of the CPA determined that oil revenues would be divided equally between southern Sudan and the Sudanese government.[8] The issue of oil was also interwoven with the sensitive issue of Sudan-China relations, which showed indications of change following the signing on the CPA.[9] Generally speaking, since the early 1990s, Chinese companies had been instrumental in turning Sudan into an oil exporter, and China was one of the Sudanese Government's more solid international allies.[10] The fact that about 75% percent of the oil production was located in the South following the CPA pushed China to tighten its relations

6 Johnson, "The Political Crisis in South Sudan," 167–9.

7 Sudd Institute, "South Sudan's Crisis: Its Drivers, Key Players, and Post-conflict Prospects," 14.

8 Patey, "Crude Days Ahead? Oil and the Resource Curse in Sudan."

9 Large, "China and South Sudan Civil War, 2013–2015."

10 For the Chinese support for the Sudanese Government stand regarding the conflict in Darfur, see: Back, *Intervention and Sovereignty in Africa: Conflict Resolution and International Organisations in Darfur*, 107–8.

with the semi-autonomous government in Juba. Salva Kiir was invited to visit China in July 2007, and the Chinese Consulate opened in Juba in September 2007. These relations grew even closer after the referendum of South Sudan in 2011. The increasingly warm relations between China and South Sudan caused considerable concern in Khartoum, which feared that it might lose the political and economic benefits of its own close relations with China. Closer relations between China and South Sudan also exacerbated corruption within the SPLA/M. According to Large,

> China was engaging a kleptocratic petro-state underpinned by military rule and the national security system, governed by the imperatives of political necessity, not competence ... Oil revenues, amounting to at least 98 percent of government revenue, allowed government salaries to be paid, with a disproportionately large proportion going to security and the SPLA.[11]

De Waal concurred that it was during the interim period that South Sudan entered into the "Kleptocratic Club," engaging in interwoven processes of increasing militarization, underdevelopment, and institutionalized corruption. As a result, despite generous per capita international funding, nearly half of all state oil revenues that flowed to the South were used to fund recurrent expenditures, militarization, and security-related projects:

> Between 2005 and 2011, the military payroll (including police and paramilitaries) expanded from 40,000 to over 300,000; salaries doubled twice; and the officer corps increased from 60 commanders to 745 generals – more than in the four US armed services combined. The political elites, meanwhile, were allowed to steal vast amounts of money – some $4 billion, according to Kiir himself.... Tragically, for all the politicians the priority was not saving their country, but personal membership in the kleptocratic club. For that privilege, they risked violence and duly reaped catastrophe.[12]

Moreover, mismanagement of public resources was not uncommon. According to Rolandsen, "South Sudan is first and foremost a subsistence economy. For ordinary people, economic interaction within the informal sector is much more important than the formal government economy."[13] In the interim period,

11 *Ibid.*, 8.
12 de Waal, "The Price of South Sudan's Independence," 195.
13 Rolandsen, "Another Civil War in South Sudan: The Failure of Guerrilla Government?" 165.

mismanagement by the leadership of the coming-into-being state was exposed in issues of oil, as well as in the use of land, South Sudan's second largest resource. de Waal claims that during the interim period, local communities increasingly lost their control over land:

> During 2007–10 alone, more than 5 percent of the land area was leased to foreign investors, ostensibly for the development of agriculture, biofuels, forestry, or wildlife parks. The deals were marked by opacity, lack of consultation with the affected communities, disregard for both customary law and the Land Act, failure of investors to deliver on promises of social services and compensation to relocated communities, and local tension.[14]

IGAD's reluctance to impose sanctions against corruption, kleptocratia, and authoritarianism by South Sudan's elites may have been related to the similar equivocation of other East African leaders, many of whom were personally involved in the mediation efforts at some point. Although IGAD's mediation efforts continued in the interim period, there seemed to be a common belief that the organization's primary role ended with the signing of the CPA.[15]

IGAD's leaders' failure to express a firm position on issues that required a clear moral stand was illustrated with respect to an incident related to the implementation of a counterpart process to the CPA in South Sudan. On March 4, 2009, the International Criminal Court (ICC) issued an arrest warrant for Sudanese President Omar al-Bashir, on charges of crimes against humanity in Darfur (the charge was subsequently changed to genocide). Although this precedential court ruling – the first arrest warrant ever issued against an incumbent head of state – prompted a very contentious debate within Africa and beyond,[16] al-Bashir was invited to participate in an extraordinary IGAD summit that was held in Nairobi in March 2010. This invitation had declarative value, as Kenya was a signatory of the Rome Statute, which formed the foundation for the ICC, and as such was obligated to arrest al-Bashir if he enters Kenyan territory.

---

14 de Waal, "When Kleptocracy Becomes Insolvent: Brute Causes of the Civil War in South Sudan," 359.

15 This recognition was acknowledged, for example, in the PSC meeting of August 2007: "[The PSC] welcomes the appointment by the Chairperson of IGAD of former President Daniel Arap Moi as Special Envoy for the CPA, in order to sustain and enhance efforts towards the full and timely implementation of the Agreement."

16 Peskin, "Caution and Confrontation in the International Criminal Court's Pursuit of Accountability in Uganda and Sudan."

Kenyan Foreign Minister Moses Wetangula stated that, "Nobody will stand in the way of President Bashir being arrested and persecuted, but for now, the AU's position is that let's see what internal mechanisms can be done. I don't think the AU is asking for too much." Adoption of the African Union's position on the ICC ruling was not surprising as the Kenyan ruling party was itself under ICC investigation at the time, for its part in post-election violence in 2007 and 2008.[17] These developments restricted the freedom of IGAD member states and their leaders to act objectively with respect to intervention in the internal affairs of other member states.

As the interim period came to a close, the 2010 elections in Sudan were another important step toward the implementation of the CPA. The first democratic local, national, and presidential elections in 24 years were originally scheduled to be held in 2009, as part of the implementation of the 2005 CPA agreement, but were ultimately held on April 16, 2010. According to official results, al-Bashir received 68.24% of the estimated 10.1 million votes. Salva Kiir's overwhelming presidential victory (92.99%) in the country's southern region was one of the most significant results of the April elections. The SPLM won 87% of the South state assembly seats as well as nine out of ten governorships.

The election results had direct consequences for the referendum in South Sudan, which was conducted on January 9, 2011, in which the population voted on whether or not to secede from the North and establish an independent state.[18] The referendum in Sudan was a watershed event of continental proportions, as the dissolution of Sudan into two sovereign states could be considered the first direct challenge to the sanctity of member states' sovereignty and territorial integrity. Notwithstanding the threat to state sovereignty, African states almost unanimously supported South Sudan's demand for self-determination at an international meeting at the United Nations in New York on September 24, 2010, which was convened by UN Secretary General Ban Ki-Moon to review the situation in advance of the referendum. African attendance at the meeting was impressive, and included the president of Malawi (chairperson of the AU), the prime minister of Ethiopia (chairperson of IGAD), other African heads of state, and representatives of other regional organizations. AU Commission Chairperson Dr. Jean Ping urged the leaders and people of Sudan to rise to the

17 *Sudan Tribune*, "Kenya Invites Bashir to IGAD Summit as he Challenges World to Arrest Him."

18 *Africa News*, "Sudan; AU Commission Chairman Urges Country to Rise to Referendum Challenge in 2011." For the relations between the election results and the referendum see: Back, *Intervention and Sovereignty in Africa*, 136–8.

historic challenge of organizing a legitimate, credible referendum on the self-determination of South Sudan. More importantly, in another Security Council meeting, representatives of both Sudan and South Sudan explicitly expressed their support for the legitimacy of the referendum:

> Both Ali Ahmed Karti, Minister for Foreign Affairs of Sudan, and Pagan Amum, Secretary-General of the Sudan People's Liberation Movement (SPLM), expressed their commitment to implementing the CPA, including holding the referendum. "The referendum is a commitment that is to be honoured and we are willing to honour it," said Mr. Karti, adding that the decision to allow the South its right to self-determination was among the more daring decisions taken in Africa. He renewed the Government's commitment to hold the referendum as scheduled and to accept the results, whether in favour of unity or secession. As for progress towards a framework agreement for the North and South, he said an historic accord had been reached yesterday on strategic issues, notably a determination not to return to war. Mr. Amum said, "The people and Government of Southern Sudan strongly desire a peaceful and collaborative relationship between the South and the North – a relationship that benefits and protects all of our peoples. Even though the people of Southern Sudan may choose to secede, we shall always remain neighbours and we have no choice but to be good neighbours." He added, "No Northern Sudanese rights will be violated or activities obstructed, regardless of the outcome of the referendum. All we ask is that the rights and livelihoods of Southern Sudanese in the North be treated in exactly the same way."[19]

The African states' unanimous support for South Sudan's insistence on its right to self-determination (and its eventual independence) was especially noteworthy in view of their rejection (and the rejection of other regional organizations) of similar claims in other cases, such as Somaliland's longstanding efforts to secede from Somalia, which are described in Chapter 6.[20] From a historical perspective, support of Southern Sudan's claim to self-determination and independence marked an almost inconceivable transformation in African perceptions since African states' independence from colonial rule.[21]

---

19 UN Security Council. "Full, Timely Implementation of Sudan's Comprehensive Peace Agreement Essential to National, Regional Stability, Security Council Presidential Statement Says."

20 Bereketeab, *Self-Determination and Secessionism in Somaliland and South Sudan: Challenges to Postcolonial State-Building.*

21 Daly, "The Sudans in the Twenty-First Century."

MAP 2 Map of South Sudan states in 2011, including Abyei
Reference: Clayton Hazvinei Vhumbunu, "Reviving peace in South Sudan through the Revitalised Peace Agreement: Understanding the enablers and possible obstacles", Conflict Trends,2018,4.Availablefrom:https://www.accord.org.za/conflict-trends/reviving-peace-in-south-sudan-through-the-revitalised-peace-agreement/

Yet, the euphoria of this important step toward South Sudan independence was beclouded by the realization of the CPA's inadequacies. Although the CPA dealt at length with political-sharing and wealth-sharing issues between the North and the South, it left unresolved many critical issues, such as the delineation of precise borders between the two states and ownership of the oil-rich area of Abyei. Although the CPA forged an innovative deal in which the two sides agreed to split the country's oil wealth, the CPA only vaguely noted that the fate of Abyei would be decided in a future referendum of Abyei inhabitants. The explosive consequences of the CPA's failure to determine the future of Abyei surfaced in the two-year period following South Sudan's independence. Although internal clashes between the region's groups had been common in the interim period, and Southern and Northern forces were involved in violent clashes in the region in May 2011,[22] tensions reached new heights, and

22 *Ibid.*, 44–54; "Sudan: Abyei Seizure by North 'Act of War,' Says South"; Back, "South Sudan, Six Months On."

IGAD renewed its mediation efforts after independence, with limited results, as described in an IPIS report:

> On 27 September 2012 a breakthrough was reached when the GRSS and the GoS signed a series of nine bilateral agreements under the auspices of the AUHIP and IGAD (Intergovernmental Authority for Development). The agreements tackled sensitive issues such as oil, security, trade and borders. The AUHIP also attempted to reach an agreement on the final status of Abyei, but its proposal was rejected by Khartoum. Despite what seemed like a diplomatic milestone, the implementation of the cooperation agreement was immediately delayed. Interstate violence flared up again in November 2012 when the SAF bombed Kiir Adem in Northern Bahr-El Ghazal for three consecutive days. It was only in March 2013 that the countries adopted an implementation matrix to facilitate the coordinated enactment of their commitments. The matrix set concrete and ambitious deadlines for each of the nine "issues" included. Again, the implementation stalled. The African Union (AU) described the stalemate as "a continuing disagreement between the Governments of Sudan and South Sudan over the implementation of the security arrangements."[23]

The informal referendum held in Abyei in October 2013, in which almost all participants voted to join South Sudan, sparked a new round of violence. Most of the voters belonged to the Ngok Dinka while other ethnic groups, such as the Arab Misseriya, who had close ties with Sudan, boycotted the referendum, and refused to recognize the results.[24] IGAD's Executive Secretary cautioned that "Such a unilateral act will not serve any positive purpose but on the contrary creates complications and tensions in an already volatile situation. The Executive Secretary of IGAD stresses that this act is not only in violation of the decisions of the African Union Peace and Security Council but also in contradiction of the framework of the existing agreements regarding Abyei." IGAD's conciliatory attitude toward the refusal to recognize the results of the referendum was a source of many future conflicts and a cause of the subsequent escalation of violence in Abyei and in South Sudan. Above all, this confirmed that it had been unrealistic to assume that the many issues that remained unclear in the CPA would eventually resolve themselves.[25]

23 Spittaels and Weyns, "Mapping Conflict Motives: The Sudan – South Sudan Border," 9.
24 "Abyei Referendum Enters Second Day."
25 "The Executive Secretary of IGAD AMB. (ENG) Mahboub M. Maalim condemns the Unilateral 'Referendum' in Abyei."

Another issue that was inadequately addressed by the CPA was South Sudan's relations with its other future neighbor states. With multiple neighbors (Ethiopia to the east, Kenya to the southeast, Uganda to the south, the Democratic Republic of the Congo to the southwest, the Central African Republic to the west), land-locked South Sudan was at risk of border disputes. As early as August 2011, a report from the border of South Sudan with its southern neighbor Uganda, for example, illustrates the complexity of the borders issue:

> Ugandan police arrested three South Sudanese citizens last month for allegedly cultivating 300 hectares of land near the village of Abaya, about 12 km inside the Ugandan border. Edward Kala, a tractor driver, Simon Jangara, his employee, and Moses Mano, a herdsman, were detained in the village of Wano and later released after the intervention of the district chief. This sparked outrage from local residents, who threatened to stage demonstrations if the issue is not resolved. At the heart of the dispute is the difference between customary boundaries, which are not legally recognised, and international borders, which date back to British colonial rule. Police investigations revealed that South Sudanese rebels had used the disputed land as a training base in the 1950s during a revolt against the Khartoum government, and had regarded it as part of southern Sudan ever since. In conversations with people on both sides of the Ugandan border, the dispute is testing the limits of patriotism, friendship and neighborly relations.[26]

The borders issue re-emerged when Uganda intervened in South Sudan's internal disputes in December 2013, which is discussed below.

The events of the first two years following independence also highlighted the fact that the most incidents that required urgent intervention were related to concerns over the unity of the new state of South Sudan. These concerns had been voiced before independence, but in 2005, after the signing of CPA, it was hoped that the SPLM/A would become a political party that would champion the unity of the people of South Sudan on a new basis, lead society to a comprehensive social transformation, and promote peaceful coexistence, equality, justice, and prosperity. Soon after independence, it became evident that the movement was hardly able to harmonize all the military factions under the SPLA.[27] The country's disjointed defense establishment was the result of the government's failure to build a professional army that reflects the

26 Moritz, "South Sudan, Uganda in Border Dilemma."

27 A note on terminology: in 2005 the SPLA/M (which later became known as the SPLM/A) was formally separated to SPLM-the political party and SPLA-the armed forces.

character and diversity of the nation: The integrated forces simply remained loyal to their former commanders turned politicians. Moreover, despite what was agreed in the CPA regarding disarmament, "The SPLA tried just one serious effort at forcible disarmament, a campaign against the 'White Army' of Jonglei in 2006. More than 2,000 people died."[28]

Besides the specific issue of disarmament, the SPLM failed the nascent state on a more crucial issue. Awolich claimed that instead of driving a major social or political transformation or articulating a new vision for an independent country, the SPLM actually deepened social and ethno-political splits and controversies[29] that had been in place prior to independence. In March 2011, after losing the election to another SPLM candidate, former SPLM General George Athor Deng led a militia that clashed with SPLM forces. After independence, the clashes between Athor – who justified his actions as a response to the undemocratic and corrupt behavior of the SPLM, and accused the ruling party of committing "crimes against humanity" against its opponents – and SPLM forces resumed in the eastern Jonglei State, claiming the lives of countless numbers of people and displacing tens of thousands, who fled their homes for the relative safety of the bush.

The growing IDPs problem was interwoven with the growing number of South Sudanese refugees who were returning to the country after independence, adding to the financial burden of the nascent state that was already struggling with a deteriorating economy. An International Alert Organization report described the situation:

> Arrival of some 360,000 South Sudanese returning from Sudan since October 2010. A further 250,000 were projected by the UN Office for the Coordination of Humanitarian Affairs (OCHA) to return during 2012, even before the March 2012 collapse in bilateral relations. This burden has fallen disproportionately on the northern states, whence they were originally displaced and which are now worst affected by the recently imposed trade blockade, as well as on urban areas. This highlights a growing economic and linguistic divide between social, regional and identity groups within the new South Sudan, with Arabic-speaking or -literate returnees from the north disadvantaged relative to English speakers returning from Kenya and Uganda, and a mismatch between economic skills and economic realities in South Sudan.[30]

28 de Waal, *The Real Politics of the Horn of Africa: Money, War and the Business of Power*, 96.
29 Awolich, "The Unwarranted Carnage in South Sudan," 1.
30 Reeve, "Peace and Conflict Assessment of South Sudan," 18.

In 2012, relations with Sudan become tense when the CPA wealth-sharing protocol governing South Sudanese oil exported by pipeline through Sudan ended. Clashes between the two countries' armies erupted around Heglig in March that year,[31] mainly because the two states were unable to reach an agreement regarding the oil flow from South Sudan to Sudan. In late January 2012, South Sudan announced that it would close oil production and exports via Port Sudan, and adopted austerity measures to counter the economic impacts of this decision, a declaration that has highlighted the extreme dependence of the South Sudan on oil revenues, and the extreme vulnerability of its economy.[32]

The general deterioration in the economic situation and populations in transition exacerbated phenomena such as cattle raiding, which proliferated in areas Eastern Equatoria, Jonglei, Lakes, Unity, Upper Nile, and Warrap states. Cattle raiding was associated with additional types of crimes, creating an absence of communal and personal security.[33] Moreover, cattle raiding was not only a national calamity in South Sudan; it tended to spill over into neighboring countries. IGAD was attentive to the problem of cattle raiding from an early stage of its existence, due to cattle's unique significance as a main source of subsistence for many citizens of South Sudan (as elsewhere in East Africa). Under its responsibility for cross-border incidents, IGAD devoted efforts to resolve this issue, for example by monitoring cattle raiding occurrences in cross-borders situations.[34] Cattle raiding incidents were also one of the factors driving the South Sudanese government's decision to launch its long-awaited national Conflict Early Warning and Response Unit (CEWERU).

The establishment of the CEWERU was part of the new state's commitment to IGAD, which had operated CEWARN since 2002, and had continued to operate it at a limited scope in South Sudan prior to 2012. The decision to expand CEWARN to a nation-wide system was welcomed by both President Kiir and his Deputy Machar, who claimed that "South Sudan, which has come out [of] a long-running civil war, continues to grapple with multiple internal and regional security challenges which necessitate a nation-wide capacity to anticipate, and act pro-actively to prevent violent conflicts." Martin Kimani, CEWARN director, viewed the establishment of CEWERU as an important milestone in advancing CEWARN's engagement in South Sudan and the wider IGAD region. He stated, "As CEWARN transitions into a new phase of operation in the post-2012

31 Ylönen, "The Sudan South Sudan Military Escalation in Heglig: Shifting Attention from Domestic Challenges."

32 Reeve, "Peace and Conflict Assessment of South Sudan," 32–4.

33 *Ibid.*, 35.

34 Personal interview with IGAD official, IGAD, Addis Ababa, August 10, 2017. See also *Sudan Tribune*, "S. Sudan Launches Conflict Early Warning and Response Unit."

period, its operations are set to expand to wider geographic and thematic areas of national and regional relevance in South Sudan as in the rest of the IGAD member states."[35] Despite the huge hopes, the new system failed to predict the eruption of the conflict in mid-December 2013, with devastating results.[36]

The year 2013 began optimistically, at least from the economic perspective. Oil production was renewed in April, albeit on a lower scale, and provided some economic relief. According to The World Bank's 2013 assessment, the economic data of South Sudan were good compared to some of its neighbors in the Horn of Africa: "Although South Sudan was starting from near zero, the country was born with a silver spoon in its mouth."[37] However, as the year progressed, internal divisions quickly deteriorated into a civil war and a humanitarian disaster.

The conflict also has a clear ethnic character, as the two rivals represent the two primary ethnic groups in South Sudan, the Dinka and the Nuer, whose deep-rooted disputes worsened following independence. Yet, ethnicity in South Sudan was much more complex than a simplistic dichotomy between these two groups, and the ethnic diversity and fragmentation were exploited by politicians to gain power in the interim period and even more so in the initial period after independence.[38]

The power struggle between President Salva Kiir and his deputy, former Vice President Riek Machar, had grown fierce since early 2013. The long-standing rivalry between Kiir and Machar was well known: Although the two fought side-by-side at times during the north-south conflict, they had wrestled over political dominance since the early 1990s,[39] and in 2008, Machar had openly announced his ambition to become president of the independent nation. After independence, Machar and several party members became more openly critical of Kiir, accusing him of heavy-handed tactics and undemocratic and dictatorial tendencies. They demanded visible progress in processes such as preparing the ground for 2015 elections and progress in the shift from the South Sudan Interim Constitution to the Transitional Constitution – which involved highly contentious political issues such as federalism, land ownership, and wider inclusion.[40]

Moreover, although Machar was once considered Khartoum's ally, tightened relations between Kiir and al-Bashir after independence, especially around

35 Julius N. Uma, "S. Sudan Launches Conflict Early Warning and Response Unit."
36 Personal interview with Dr. Sunday Okello, African Union Peace and Security Programme.
37 de Waal, *The Real Politics of the Horn of Africa: Money, War and the Business of Power*, 100.
38 Johnson, "Briefing: The Crisis in South Sudan."
39 de Waal, "The Price of South Sudan's Independence," 195.
40 Personal interview with IGAD official, Addis Ababa, August 10, 2017.

common interests on the oil production, led to a gradual decline in Machar's power and dismissal of his supporters from influential positions (along with members of Garang's old echelons). On July 23, Kiir fired Machar and the entire presidential cabinet, and temporarily suspended SPLM Secretary General Pagan Amum, who was considered a hardliner against Khartoum.[41]

In the second half of 2013, several opposition groups organized a large public rally scheduled for December 13. The rally was postponed when the groups hoped that a meeting of the SPLM National Liberation Council (NLC; a body composed of 150 elders from across South Sudan) would reach agreements on key issues such as leadership and constitution. The national leadership once again failed to integrate civil society groups into the conflict resolution efforts. Not only did the political elites lack commitment to a true integration of civil society in these processes, but the civil society groups themselves reflected the splits and divisions of their society and were struggling to find a common denominator.[42]

On December 15, shots were fired for unknown reasons at the army headquarters after SPLM's ruling committee meeting ended in deadlock, and fighting erupted between government forces and those loyal to Machar. Both Kiir and Machar accused each other of initiating the violence; Kiir accused Machar and his followers of attempting a coup-d'état, while Machar accused Kiir of voicing false accusations and attempting to dispose of him and his supporters. On the ground, violence rapidly spread in Juba and then, to the rest of the country, as reported in a UN Human Rights Division report:

> Fighting subsequently spread to the Sudan People's Liberation Army (SPLA) headquarters and an armory, and by 16 December, gunfire was reported throughout Juba, with massive violence and consequent population displacements … in the subsequent days, fighting spread to Jonglei, Unity and the Upper Nile states, and Mr. Machar declared its intention to bring down the Government under President Kiir's leadership. Opposition forces took control of the capitals of Jonglei, Upper Nile and Unity states … heavy fighting ensued as the towns of Bor, Malakal, and Benitu changed hands several times in the late December through mid-January. Although a cessation of hostilities agreement was signed by the GRSS and the SPLM/Army in Opposition on 23 January 2014, UNMISS

41 Johnson, "The Political Crisis in South Sudan," 169–71.

42 CCR, "The Peacebuilding Role of Civil Society in South Sudan," 9–13.

> continues to receive reports of fighting in parts of Jonglei, Unity and Upper Nile states.[43]

According to Alex de Waal, "On 15 December, the friction of the political contest generated just such a spark, and within two days the whole edifice of government, party, and army was blown apart. The 2006 Juba Agreement, the basis of internal stability in South Sudan, was dead."[44] de Waal described how the SPLM in Opposition, the new movement created by Machar following the split with Kiir, mobilized the "White Army" of Nuer youth and how their clashes with the Government forces (assisted by Ugandan troops, as described below), immediately led to an escalation of the conflict on the ground.

Arguably, IGAD's response to the escalating conflict reflected both the weaknesses and the strengths of its mediation abilities. On the one hand, IGAD responded immediately to the eruption of the South Sudanese crisis. Within four days, its representatives arrived in Juba, along with other representatives from the AU, the UN, and other international organizations. Very soon after, on December 27, 2013, IGAD convened a summit of heads of states and government in Nairobi, urging the AU Peace and Security Council and the international community to intervene immediately. IGAD also demanded that the AU organs that deal with human rights violations to establish a commission to investigate the incidents and submit its findings within three months. The organization's swift and firm response was noted in a report by International Crisis Group:

> The regional organisation, the Inter-Governmental Authority on Development (IGAD), responded quickly. Three envoys, Ambassador Seyoum Mesfin (Ethiopia), General Lazarus Sumbeiywo (Kenya) and General Mohammed Ahmed Mustafa al-Dhabi (Sudan) shuttled between Juba, Addis Ababa, where peace talks have been held, and opposition-controlled territory and, after weeks of pressure and negotiation, obtained a cessation of hostilities. However, this was violated almost immediately, and fighting continues, as a monitoring and verification mission struggles to establish itself on the ground. Neighbouring Uganda (also an IGAD member), as well as forces associated with Sudanese armed opposition groups,

43 United Nations Mission in South Sudan (UNMISS). Interim Report on Human Rights: Crisis in South Sudan, 5–6.

44 de Waal, "When Kleptocracy Becomes Insolvent," 366. For a detailed discussion on the 2006 Juba declaration, see: Young, "The South Sudan Defence Forces in the Wake of the Juba Declaration."

> notably the Justice and Equality Movement (JEM), intervened early in support of the South Sudanese government. That in turn may yet trigger Sudan government support to the SPLA in Opposition. Announced plans for an IGAD-led force,[45] about which there are critical mandate, composition and funding questions, raises the prospect of even greater regional involvement in the civil war.[46]

One of the most specific agreements brokered by IGAD concerned the status of the detainees. The agreement was signed between the Government of the Republic of South Sudan (GRSS) and representatives of SPLM/A-IO, "recognizing that both parties acknowledge the role that the detainees can play in the ongoing dialogue of South Sudan."[47] The IGAD Special Envoys Chair, Ambassador Seyoum Mesfin, stated that the signing of the agreements were an important milestone in the IGAD-led mediation process in pursuit of a peaceful political solution to the crisis that gripped the Republic of South Sudan.[48]

Efforts were also expanded to intervene more significantly on the ground. In addition to the decision to create a protection and deterrent force within UNMISS, with troops from Ethiopia, Kenya, and Rwanda, IGAD heads of states adopted measures such as asset freezes, travel bans, and arms embargo, and pledged to "take the necessary measures to directly intervene in South Sudan to protect life and restore peace and stability."[49] de Waal claims that, "This was not mediation understood as assisting the warring parties to come to agreement, but rather the imposition of a new level of militarized regional governance on South Sudan."[50]

Nonetheless, the deep mutual distrust between Kiir and Machar prevented IGAD from brokering a power-sharing arrangement between them. Time after time, agreements were signed and violated: The agreements brokered by IGAD in January 2014, including a ceasefire agreement and agreements to establish various mechanisms to ensure its implementation, such as the Monitoring Verification Mechanism (MVM), were repeatedly violated, and the parties

45 *Africa Research Bulletin*, "IGAD Decision on South Sudan Force."
46 International Crisis Group, "South Sudan: A Civil War by Any Other Name," 3.
47 Agreement on the Status of Detainees between the Government of the Republic of South Sudan (GRSS) and the Sudan People's Liberation Movement/Army (In-Opposition) SPLM/A (In-Opposition).
48 *Reliefweb*, "South Sudanese Parties Sign Agreements on Cessation of Hostilities and Question of Detainees."
49 Resolutions by the 28th Extraordinary Summit of the IGAD Heads of State and Government.
50 de Waal, *The Real Politics of the Horn of Africa*, 107.

suffered no consequences. Other agreements brokered by IGAD that year (for example in May and August) also failed to be implemented.[51] Not only were the parties distrustful of each other, they were also suspicious of the intentions of IGAD and other regional and international organizations. Machar accused IGAD (and more broadly the AU) of favoritism towards the existing ruling party, while President Kiir accused the United Nations Mission in South Sudan (UNMISS) of supporting the rebels' cause.

IGAD's limited authority to force a solution was evident from its inability to prevent the military intervention of one of its member states in the territory of another member state. Indeed, Uganda, a member of IGAD, had deployed its troops in South Sudan immediately after the conflict broke out[52] and Ugandan troops were involved in active combat against the rebels in Jonglei, Upper Nile, and Unity States.[53] Uganda even claimed that the rebels had been close to taking control of Juba had it not been for the intervention of Ugandan army. Well-known scholar and political commentator Mahmood Mamdani commented on IGAD's inability to curtail the Ugandan intervention in South Sudan:

> The internal reality is that reform will have to be imposed on a reluctant Salva Kiir from the outside, most obviously, IGAD. The external reality is that the reform is also likely to be opposed by Uganda. Convinced that the solution in South Sudan must be military, not political, the Ugandan government has staked troops, estimated at around 4,500, to make a military solution possible. The government admits that without their intervention, the Salva Kiir government would have fallen in a matter of days. The regional rivals, Uganda and Sudan, were the first to come to Salva Kiir's assistance. Could it be that the desire to preempt a stronger involvement by Sudan led to Uganda's hasty commitment of troops inside South Sudan?[54]

Mamdani, who proposed that efforts to resolve the crisis might benefit from the lessons of history, stated,

51 Bereketeab, "The Collapse of IGAD Peace Mediation in the Current South Sudan Civil War," 151–2.

52 Apuuli, "IGAD's Mediation in the Current South Sudan Conflict: Prospects and Challenges," 128–30.

53 Bereketeab, "The Collapse of IGAD Peace Mediation in the Current South Sudan Civil War," 148.

54 Mamdani, "Prof. Mamdani Speech on S. Sudan: Part II."

> Both the UN and IGAD need to take a lesson from the Democratic Republic of Congo, where it became clear over time that a political solution would require the introduction of forces from countries without a direct political stake in Kivu (in this case, South Africa and Tanzania, as opposed to Rwanda and Uganda). In South Sudan too, the way forward calls for the replacement of Ugandan troops with troops from other countries in the region, countries without a direct political stake in South Sudan and with a mandate and a political will to oversee the implementation of a necessary political reform.

In a press briefing in response to this call, the Ugandan Government reiterated its commitment to IGAD's mediation efforts and commitment to defend to its own interests:

> Uganda is a member state of Intergovernmental Authority on Development (IGAD) and therefore fully subscribes and supports the ongoing peace talks in Addis Ababa under the mediation of IGAD. This peace process was initiated by the IGAD Heads of State and Government who held an Extra-Ordinary Session on 27th December, 2013, in Nairobi to discuss the situation in South Sudan. In part, the communique of the Heads of State commended the efforts of the Republic of Uganda in securing critical infrastructure and installations in South Sudan, and pledged its support to these efforts.[55]

By the end of 2014, South Sudan had become "a hive of regional rivalries."[56] On the ground, the Ugandan military intervention continued, and Sudan, motivated by its desire to protect its oil flow from South Sudan, became actively involved in the internal political struggles. Ethiopia and Kenya contributed forces to UNMISS, in order to strengthen their positions as regional powers.

Yet, even as conditions on the ground deteriorated rapidly, international and regional actors called upon IGAD to once again apply its previous mediation experience, and in particular its experience in cooperating with international partners. The EU, for example, increased its efforts to participate in the mediation efforts, and expressed its desire to increase the cooperation with IGAD:

55 Republic of Uganda, Press Briefing by Hon. Sam K. Kutesa, Minister of Foreign Affairs, regarding South Sudan.

56 de Waal, "The Price of South Sudan's Independence," 196.

> The EU firmly supports the tireless efforts of IGAD and its mediators to bring an end to the suffering in South Sudan. The EU is assisting IGAD both in substantive and financial terms and is contributing staff to the ceasefire monitoring and verification mechanism. Supporting IGAD in its efforts to mediate between the warring parties and broker a peaceful solution to the conflict. €1.1 million have been mobilized from the EU's African Peace Facility to allow IGAD to set up a platform for peace talks and provide initial funding to a monitoring and verification mechanism. The EU is considering extending this support.[57]

The violence had a devastating effect on the newborn state. By the end of January 2014, an estimated 740,000 persons became IDPs in South Sudan, and others fled to neighboring countries. Evidence of grave human rights violations, including murder and gender-based crimes came to light. In 2015, after less than two years of independence, tens of thousands of people were believed to have been killed in the bloodshed. Of a total population of 12 million, 1.4 million people became displaced inside the country, nearly half a million sought refuge outside the country, and almost the entire population of South Sudan was at some risk of famine.[58]

The constant deterioration of the humanitarian situation was a major factor in the prevailing assumption that IGAD's days of glory as a mediator between rival parties in East Africa were over. The South Sudan News Agency (SSNA) reported that IGAD-led negotiations "have become part of recurrent jokes among many leaders of the African Union."[59] de Waal claimed, "IGAD, designated as mediator, adopted a peacemaking formula based on reflex rather than reflection."[60] Yet, despite the fact that IGAD's abilities to conduct an effective mediation process were questionable at the time, the need for its mediation experience and abilities was required again in the next few years, as discussed in the next chapter.

57 European Union, "Factsheet: The EU and South Sudan."
58 See, for example: UN, "Uprooted by Conflict: South Sudan's Displacement Crisis."
59 *South Sudan News Agency*, "Exclusive: IGAD-led Peace Talks are not Convincing."
60 de Waal, "The Price of South Sudan's Independence," 196.

CHAPTER 5

Winter of Despair? IGAD's Mediation Efforts 2015–2018

The escalating conflict in South Sudan had horrific consequences on the country's population. According to UN estimations, 200,000 children were at a risk of severe famine, and 50,000 would face imminent death if food aid did not arrive urgently. Together with the rapidly growing numbers of IDPs (estimated around 2.5 million at the time) and refugees, IGAD experts estimated that $ 1.6 billion was required in order to relieve the situation: "IGAD believed that though this is not a small amount, it is not beyond the capacity of all those who are ready and willing to assist to the people of South Sudan."[1]

Fighting continued through 2015, despite IGAD's mediation efforts to create stability-promoting mechanisms such as the Memorandum on the Cessation of Hostilities that was signed in January 2014, and the situation deteriorated rapidly. During the dry season of 2015, violence that was initially limited to the Greater Upper Nile began to spread to other regions. South Sudan's oil fields were repeatedly attacked, and reduced oil production had harsh financial effects on the new state's fragile economy and its credibility, as described in the *Wall Street Journal*:

> Seeking to keep their cash-strapped government afloat, South Sudan officials huddled in June in Juba with Chinese, Malaysian and Indian oil executives to propose an emergency loan of $200 million, according to participants in the meeting. As they made the appeal, officials shared some other unwelcome news: South Sudan couldn't pay back the $1.6 billion it had already borrowed from these companies. We can't afford to service our debts at the moment, Finance Minister Aggrey Tisa Sabuni said to the group, according to a South Sudanese official who attended the meeting. "Unfortunately this is a situation we cannot get out easily without more advance payments."[2]

1 "South Sudan-IGAD Warning."

2 Nicholas Bariyo, "South Sudan's Debt Rises as Oil Ebbs: Oil Companies No Longer Want to Extend Advance Payments."

 | DOI:10.1163/9789004425323_007

South Sudanese politicians seemed not to make a connection between the deteriorating economic situation and the country's political instability. In effect, the gulf between political parties continued to widen, and identity politics intensified. Besides the well-known rivalry between Kiir and Machar, who represented the SPLM and the SPLM-IO, respectively, additional opposition groups, such as SPLM-Former Detainees, known also as G11, emerged constantly. To complicate the situation even further, several South Sudanese political leaders retained their ties to former SPLM fighters situated outside the borders of South Sudan, specifically in the three contested areas (South Kordofan, the Blue Nile, and Abyei).[3] These cross-border associations not only worsened the internal conflict within South Sudan, but also threatened its relations with its northern neighbor, as discussed below.[4]

Concerns that a dead-end in the mediation process would lead to further escalation on ground were expressed at a joint meeting of the AU Peace and Security Council and the UN Security Council, where the risks of imposing sanctions on the rival parties was also discussed:

> The AUPSC and the members of the UNSC urged the parties to recommit to an unconditional end to hostilities as provided for in the Cessation of Hostilities Agreement, as well as to negotiate in good faith and without preconditions and conclude their consultations on outstanding matters, with particular focus on the establishment and structure of the Transitional Government of National Unity as soon as possible. In this respect, they reiterated their determination to impose sanctions against all parties that threaten the peace, security or stability of South Sudan, in particular those who continue to undermine the Cessation of Hostilities Agreement and obstruct the political process, in line with their relevant pronouncements in support to the communiqué of the IGAD 28th Extraordinary Summit and UNSC resolution 2206 (2015).[5]

Indeed, in March 2015, following fifteen months of unsuccessful mediation efforts, IGAD announced a revised, expanded mediation process that became

3 Leach, *War and Politics in Sudan: Cultural Identities and the Challenge of the Peace Process*, 78–9.

4 Rolandsen. "Another Civil War in South Sudan: The Failure of Guerrilla Government?" 167–9.

5 9th Annual Joint Consultative Meeting between African Union Peace and Security Council (AUPSC) and the United Nation Security Council (UNSC).

known as "IGAD-PLUS."[6] The revised process was intended to create a unified international front based on the active participation of partners, including the AU, UN, EU, China, United States, Britain, Norway, and IGAD Partners Forum.[7] It also was designed to promote discussions of important issues such as the basis of the power-sharing ratio, transitional governance, and security agreements. It encouraged the UN to appoint a dedicated envoy to South Sudan and Sudan, with a political role distinct from the peacekeeping mission, to represent the UN in IGAD-PLUS on issues such as working with member states and with the UN's sanctions committee to ensure the effectiveness of the sanctions. IGAD-PLUS also extended the AU's involvement in the mediation process, by encouraging the appointment of an ad hoc high-level committee of five heads of states and a high-ranking representative for South Sudan (former Malian President Alpha Oumar Konaré), to resolve the regional rivalries that hampered the mediation efforts. In his opening statement Ethiopian Prime Minister Hailemariam Desalegn, then-chairperson of IGAD, declared:

> Toward the end of July 2015, we the IGAD-PLUS, shared with you a Proposed Compromise Agreement on the Resolution of the Conflict in South Sudan. As I noted then, the proposal drew on the extensive negotiations that you have had ever since we began meeting here in Addis Ababa, in January 2014. Drawing on your own discussions, negotiations and suggestions, we attempted to capture the emerging ideas, concerns, and interests. We, the IGAD Envoys and the IGAD-PLUS representatives, believe that, if implemented wholeheartedly in a letter and spirit, the Compromise Agreement can take the stakeholders, and the entire people of South Sudan to a better future. As we requested you to undertake further consultations with your respective leaderships and constituencies on the proposals, it is our hope that you have had enough time to consult, since the proposals are the very same issues that you have been discussing for the last 19 months. We all do believe that South Sudan is undergoing trying times by mere virtue of your presence here. I dare say, also, that we do agree on the contours of the solutions to those challenges except in the nuances.[8]

6 Actually, this initiative was born already in January 2015, as IGAD came with a proposal of power-sharing between the two rivals that will allow Kiir to stay in power and Machar to resume his vice president position. See: Bereketeab, "Why South Sudan Conflict is Proving Intractable."

7 International Crisis Group, "South Sudan: Keeping Faith with the IGAD Peace Process."

8 Opening Statement by the Chairperson of the IGAD Special Envoys for South Sudan; "LATEST: IGAD Special Envoys Congratulate South Sudan on Peace Signing."

IGAD was one of the driving forces behind the peace agreement that was signed on August 17, 2015. Despite objections and delays, mainly on Kiir's part,[9] a power-sharing formula was signed between the government, the armed opposition, former political detainees, and other stakeholders in the country. The agreement included clauses on permanent ceasefire and transitional security arrangements, and called for the establishment of the Transitional Government of National Unity of the Republic of South Sudan (TGoNU).[10]

The agreement also included a decision to establish the Joint Monitoring and Evaluation Commission (JMEC), which was considered as a vital mechanism that would encourage and support the South Sudan signatory parties in implementing the agreement, The JMEC, comprised

> the parties, key South Sudanese stakeholders, IGAD member states, the AU, and the broader international community, would monitor the implementation of the agreement and its key reforms. The JMEC would be chaired by an eminent African and report on implementation progress every three months to the AU Peace and Security Council, UN Security Council, IGAD, UN Secretary-General, AU Chairperson, and the transitional government. The Chair of JMEC could also report to those bodies at any time and recommend remedial action if the agreement was not being implemented.[11]

IGAD appointed the former Botswana President Festus Mogae as the head of the new commission.[12] The JMEC attracted many hopes, especially in view of its exclusive mandate to monitor and take action to control the escalation of the conflicts on ground.

Among the many chapters of the August 2015 Agreement, the chapter on transitional justice, accountability, reconciliation, and healing is of special interest.[13] References to the case of Rwanda confirmed the historical significance of the 1994 genocide in Rwanda as a turning point in continental attitudes toward intrastate conflicts and a warning sign for other similar cases. Indeed,

9 Even IGAD mediators themselves announced a definitive breakdown in the peace talks in March 2015; see: de Waal, "The Price of South Sudan's Independence," 196.

10 IGAD, "Agreement on the Resolution of the Conflict in the Republic of South Sudan," 5–19, 20–6.

11 IGAD, "JMEC Agreement Summary."

12 *Sudan Tribune*, "IGAD appoints former Botswana President to Head Monitoring Commission on South Sudan"; Interview with Mearuf Nurhusein, IGAD, Addis Ababa, August 10, 2017.

13 IGAD, "Agreement on the Resolution of the Conflict in the Republic of South Sudan," 40–5.

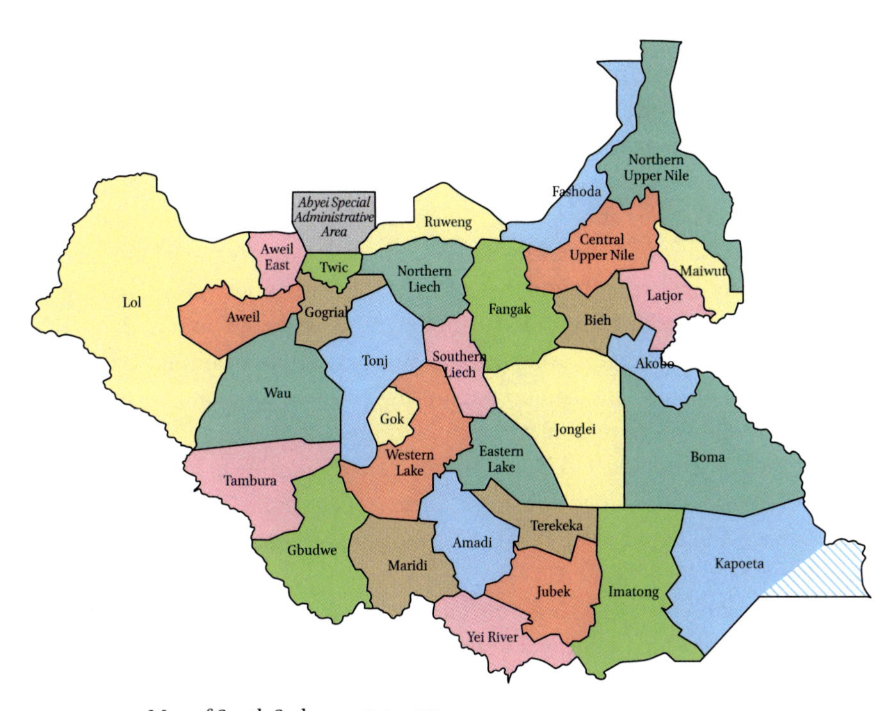

MAP 3 Map of South Sudan 32 states 2019
Reference: From Wikimedia Commons, the free media repository. Available from: https://www.google.co.il/search?hl=en&tbm=isch&source=hp&biw=1920&bih=969&ei=tB5eXpe2Jc38kwXb66PABA&q=igad+south+sudan+maps&oq=igad+south+sudan+maps&gs_l=img.3...1007.9879..10231...0.0..0.225.2214.12j8j1......0....1..gws-wiz-img.......0j0i8i30j0i24._HvVZIPcjls&ved=0ahUKEwiX4J3A-v3nAhVN_qQKHdv1CEgQ4dUDCAY&uact=5#imgrc=cLikRdVD5vHmTM&imgdii=d8GWnEU4nKU5wM

already in 2014, several observers compared the situation in South Sudan to the case of Rwanda two decades earlier.[14] Yet, Rwanda was not merely a warning, its post-genocidal rehabilitation policy served as a model for other African states suffering from internal conflicts. In this vein, the 2015 agreement provided for the establishment of a Hybrid Court for South Sudan (HCSS) that would investigate and persecute individuals responsible for violations of international or South Sudanese laws after December 2013. The agreement was very detailed on various issues, such as cooperation with other transitional justice mechanisms, the abolition of the death penalty as a possible penalty, yet none of these decisions seem to have been actually implemented.

14 Sengupta, "In South Sudan, Some Lessons of Rwanda Learned, Others Revisited." Rolandsen, "Another Civil War in South Sudan: The Failure of Guerrilla Government," 164, claims that those references were made in order to add some extra drama. Since then, however, the claims about genocide in South Sudan were sounded more often.

Already in 2014, a report of the African Union Commission of Inquiry on South Sudan (AUCISS) noted that "South[ern] Sudan has experienced numerous episodes of violations of human rights. However ... lack of capacity as well an official policy that privileged peace and stability ... have resulted in a seemingly entrenched culture of impunity."[15] A 2016 Amnesty International report reinforced the claims that human rights violations, disregard of legalization issues, and a culture of impunity had become increasingly prevalent in South Sudan. According to that report, the seeds of these phenomena had been sown in the interim period: They took root in the initial years of South Sudan's independence, and worsened during the civil war period. For example, in February 2015, "President Kiir issued an order granting amnesty to all those 'waging war against the state,' with no limitations with respect to crimes against humanity, war crimes or genocide."[16] The report advised the parties to learn from other cases of hybrid justice mechanisms in Africa (such as the Special Court for Sierra Leone) and beyond (such as the Extraordinary Chambers in the Courts of Cambodia).[17]

Unfortunately, events in late 2015 and the beginnings of 2016 indicated that instead of looking for solutions of the deteriorating situation, such as the establishment of viable justice systems, the South Sudanese rivals had no intention of accepting the terms of the 2015 agreement: They were focused on making the most of opportunities to strengthen their positions.[18] Kiir, for example, attempted to remap the South Sudan federal system by carving the country into 28 regional states instead of ten. While he argued that the new distribution would improve government control from Juba to the provinces, Machar claimed that this step was a violation of the CPA's power-sharing agreement, which called for the inclusion of the federated system into a new permanent constitution.[19]

Although the 2015 agreement called for the demilitarization of Juba and its surroundings, and despite the decision to unite the two rival military forces, in practice the two rival forces continued to exist and fight. Their failure to

15 Final Report of the African Union Commission of Inquiry on South Sudan – Executive Summary.

16 Amnesty International, "Looking for Justice: Recommendations for the Establishment of the Hybrid Court for South Sudan," 8.

17 *Ibid.*, 11–19. Unfortunately, it seemed that these recommendations were not implemented and even completely ignored to date. One recent example was President Kiir's decision to sentence Machar's spokesman to death, despite internal and global condemnations. See: Dumo, "South Sudan Sentences Rebel Leader's Spokesman to Death."

18 Knopf, "Ending South Sudan's Civil War."

19 The deadline for implementing the decision was January 2016, but in fact this decision has still not been implemented. See: Roach, "South Sudan: A Volatile Dynamic of Accountability and Peace," 1352–53.

implement such a fundamental component of the agreement was highly explosive in the fragile conditions that existed in the capital and its vicinity.[20]

In February 2016, in response to heavy pressure brought to bear by the United States and the UN, Kiir asked Machar to return to Juba, where he appointed him as the first Vice President. In late April, Machar returned to Juba and assumed his former position. In July 2016, what was supposed to be the ushering in of a renewed national unity government collapsed, after military clashes erupted between soldiers loyal to Kiir and those loyal to Machar, who fled Juba after the resumption of violence.[21] Machar went into exile once again, and Kiir replaced him with General Taban Deng Gai, another politician of Nuer origin. This move divided the SPLM/A-IO into two armed factions.[22]

The fighting was not limited to the two parties that signed the peace agreement, and other rebel forces, such as the Arrow Boys in Western Equatoria, the Cobra Squad of David YauYau, and a splinter group of Machar SPLM-IO, led by General Peter Gardet, contributed to the general deterioration.[23] Several of these groups operated within South Sudan, while others were active beyond its borders – the latter fueled created fears that the South Sudanese conflict would spill over to its neighboring countries.[24]

In Ethiopia's Gambela Region, for example, the conflict in neighboring South Sudan stimulated interethnic tensions between the Anuak and Nuer people, as their counterparts from South Sudan began to arrive there in growing numbers. Ethiopian Nuer had joined their kin fighting in South Sudan, and there was a widespread perception that the state government in Gambela was sympathetic to the Nuer-dominated SPLM/A-IO. The two adjacent regions shared ethnic ties as well as economic interests in trade and infrastructure development, as the Gambela Region was also considered the site of significant foreign investments in large-scale agriculture schemes. The deteriorating situation in the areas bordering on South Sudan led Ethiopian Prime Minister Hailemariam Desalegn to declare, "We will not support an armed struggling group or anyone who opts for path of war therefore we will not allow any armed movement which is detracting from peace in our region both in Ethiopia and

20 Interview with Mearuf Nurhusein, IGAD, Addis Ababa, August 10, 2017.

21 Githigaro, "What Went Wrong in South Sudan in December 2013?" 120–1.

22 Dessu, "IGAD's Initiative is Encouraging, but it's Unlikely to Overcome Obstacles that have Bedeviled Previous Efforts."

23 Oluoch, "What Prospects for a Lasting Peace in South Sudan?" For an elaborated discussion on the various splits of the militias in South Sudan, see: Stringham and Forney, "It Takes a Village to Raise a Militia: Local Politics, the Nuer White Army, and South Sudan's Civil Wars," 182–3.

24 Interview with Dr. Sunday Okello, African Union Peace and Security Programme.

South Sudan."[25] As the situation in the border area deteriorated further, Ethiopians deployed troops to South Sudan in April 2016.[26]

The case of Uganda was slightly different in view of Ugandan troops' involvement on the ground in South Sudan since 2013. Uganda was nonetheless surprised by several of the effects of this involvement, such as the emergence of new armed rebel groups in the Equatoria region of South Sudan that were recruiting young people of a similar ethnic background from northern Uganda, and the continued flow of light weapons across the border between the two states.[27] As for Kenya, escalating violence in South Sudan affected the continuing flow of refugees to the over-populated refugee camps in Kenya, and aggravated feelings of insecurity in the border area between the two states, as described below.

Thus, by mid-2016, the hopes that rallied around the 2015 agreement and Machar's return to Juba had been shattered, and South Sudan's neighbors and the international community grew increasingly concerned about the situation in South Sudan. The humanitarian crisis in South Sudan was considered one of the worst in the world, and was compared to the crises in Syria, Afghanistan, and Somalia. In addition to the soaring numbers of refugees and IDPs, approximately 40 percent of the population faced severe food shortage, and approximately 75 percent faced some degree of food insecurity. These were the highest levels of famine and food insecurity estimated since the outbreak of the war in 2013.[28]

In his July 2016 visit to Kigali, Rwanda, UN Secretary-General Ban Ki-Moon expressed his deep concerns over the situation in South Sudan. In his meeting with several leaders from IGAD countries, he voiced his concerns over the rising levels of sexual violence in South Sudan and incidents such as the SPLA's looting of the UN Food Programme warehouse, which had contained food assistance for approximately 220,000 people. He stressed the need to stop the violence and force the South Sudanese leaders to "sit down together and make a firm confirmation that they will work as one team, the President and First

25 Quoted in Bereketeab, "The Collapse of IGAD Peace Mediation in the Current South Sudan Civil War," 160.

26 Interview with Dr. Sunday Okello. It is important to mention that the relations between South Sudan and the Gambela Region were deep-rooted, and for a long period SPLM/A operated its radio station from there.

27 Bereketeab, "The Collapse of IGAD Peace Mediation in the Current South Sudan Civil War," 160.

28 OCHA, *South Sudan Humanitarian Bulletin*.

Vice-President."[29] As violence continued through the end of 2016, the Security Council voted to increase UNMISS troop levels through a Regional Protection Force originally proposed by IGAD, and to prioritize UNMISS resources allocated to protect civilians. The Security Council also considered a draft resolution on imposing an arms embargo and additional targeted sanctions on SPLM/A and SPLM/A-IO forces in December 2016.[30]

These worries were echoed in the communiqué of the IGAD Extra-Ordinary Summit on the situation of South Sudan, that convened the following next month in Addis Ababa:

> [The Summit] Reiterates its condemnation in strongest terms the fighting that broke out in Juba on 8th July 2016 between the guards of the former First Vice President and the presidential guards in the Presidential Palace (J1) resulting in huge loss of lives, displacement of the civilian population and destruction of property, also condemns the reported widespread sexual violence, including rape of women and young girls by armed men in uniform. In this respect, reiterates its call for an urgent in-depth independent investigation by the African Union on the fighting that took place in Juba and to identify those responsible with a view of ensuring that they are held accountable for their criminal acts.[31]

In response, IGAD promised to renew its mediation efforts in the South Sudan civil war, although the atmosphere in the second half of 2016 and early 2017 was one of despair.[32] South Sudan's economy deteriorated dramatically in 2016, as the government struggled to respond to the global drop in oil prices and borrowed heavily to fight the war. According to Crisis Group Africa's report, the growing debt triggered hyperinflation, which, combined with a severe drought (that affected the entire region of East Africa), contributed to a 40 percent decline in national food production compared to the February-April period in the previous year.[33]

29 UN, "Ban Welcomes New Agreement with Inter Parliamentary Union; Reiterates Concern at South Sudan Crisis."

30 This resolution, however, "failed due to abstentions from China, Russia, and six other countries who claimed that the South Sudanese government was showing promising signs of engagement in the peace process." See: Genser, "The United Nations Security Council's Implementation of the Responsibility to Protect," 468–9.

31 IGAD, "Communiqué of the Second IGAD PLUS Extraordinary Summit on the Situation in the Republic of South Sudan." Another clause of the Communiqué condemned the attack on aid workers and the looting of the UN humanitarian stores.

32 Gettelman, "War Consumes South Sudan, a Young Nation Cracking Apart."

33 Crisis Group Africa, "Instruments of Pain (II): Conflict and Famine," 3–4.

Indeed, as the fighting spread to new areas, famine engulfed areas that were traditionally known for their rich agriculture and natural resources. All the while, new armed groups continued to emerge, "making the political landscape extremely messy."[34] Moreover, accusations of ethnic cleansing,[35] and even possible "Rwandan-style genocide," were frequently hurled at both the government and the rebel troops, adding to South Sudan's disintegrating reputation. By early 2017, the humanitarian crisis involved 1.9 million IDPs and 1.8 million refugees. Some reports indicated that in the periods of heavy fighting, 2,500 people were fleeing daily to Uganda and many others to Ethiopia and Sudan.[36] The soaring number of refugees from South Sudan imposed a heavy burden for all the countries in IGAD region, which already suffered from a severe refugee problem.

Already in 2015, the "IGAD region hosted 12% and produced 15% of the world's refugees, carrying far more than its share in the global burden. As the fifth largest host, Ethiopia alone hosts 665,000 refugees."[37] In 2009, IGAD's efforts to formulate a regional migration policy framework, for example by defining different status for voluntary and involuntary migration, or defining protocols for free movement of people, were largely unsuccessful.[38] The escalation of the conflict in South Sudan since July 2015, however, created a heavy and unexpected burden of refugees for other IGAD countries. This burden, coupled with other regional threats, was recognized as one of the major risks to the region's stability, as the following official Kenyan bulletin stated:

> The region has borne a heavy burden of the conflict including the intensive flow of refugees, loss of investments and business as well as proliferation of small arms and light weapons from the conflicts in South Sudan and Somalia. These pose serious threats to regional peace and stability. In the case of South Sudan, Kenya continues to engage towards the secession of hostilities and implementation of the Agreement on the Resolution of the Conflict.[39]

34 Bereketeab, "The Collapse of IGAD Peace Mediation," 157.

35 Sandu. "The South Sudan Coup: A Political Rivalry that Turned Ethnic."

36 *Ibid.*, 51.

37 Maru, "Migration Priorities and Normative and Institutional Framework in the IGAD Region," 5. See also: Maru, "IGAD – Migration Action Plan (MAP) to Operationalize the IGAD Regional Migration Policy Framework (IGAD-RMPF) 2015–2020."

38 *Ibid.*, 8–10.

39 "Kenya Focus on Peace and Security in the Horn of Africa."

It quickly became clear that no significant improvement could be expected in 2017: Violence and famine continued to worsen, and spread to new, formerly peaceful areas. Moreover, traditional prevalent practices such as cattle raiding became an instrument of political violence. The rivaling parties inflamed traditional rivalries of ethnic groups, such as the Murle and the Luo Nuer, around issues of cattle raiding, and the escalation on the ground caused growing numbers of casualties, both within South Sudan and across its borders. In March 2017, for example, Ethiopian officials reported that 28 people had died and 28 children had been abducted from Nuer villages in Gambela as a result of cattle raiding committed by Murle gunmen from South Sudan.[40] As cross-borders issues and pastoral community activities were considered IGAD's special expertise and purview, the mounting frequency and violence of the cattle-raiding incidents compelled the organization to devise a more significant intervention.[41]

At the IGAD Summit of Heads of States, which convened in Addis Ababa in June 2017, the gravity of the situation propelled IGAD leaders to call upon the rival parties of South Sudan to draw up a plan and a timetable to revitalize the 2015 peace agreement. Although most of IGAD's Heads of States attended the summit, Kiir did not. Instead, he sent Taban Deng, although the latter's position as First Vice President was unacceptable to many. According to Bronwyn Bruton, an analyst at the Atlantic Council's Africa Center, "The fact that Salva Kiir has not bothered to come and speak to his colleagues in IGAD, at a time when South Sudan is falling apart and when his inability to protect his citizens is causing a refugee crisis throughout the entire region, his failure to show up, I think speaks volumes about the source of the problems in South Sudan."[42]

The need to integrate civil society representatives in an inclusive national dialogue was also noted by the David Shearer, UN Special Representative of the Secretary-General to the 2017 IGAD Summit. He mentioned that during his travels in South Sudan he witnessed the valuable work of local organizations,

40 Wild, Jok, and Pate, "The Militarization of Cattle Raiding in South Sudan: How a Traditional Practice Became a Tool for Political Violence," 1.

41 Interview with IGAD official, IGAD, Addis Ababa, 10 August 2017. According to that official, issues of cross-border cattle raiding are particularly complex, as they involve aspects such as sovereignty of states. In this regard, the role of IGAD, as a regional organization, in actions such as checking the accuracy of the reports from both sides, is particularly significant.

42 According to South Sudan presidential spokesperson Ateny Wek Ateny: "The president did not attend the summit because the IGAD summit has coincided with other commitments of the same equal importance. Like in any sovereign state, the president sent his first vice president, Taban Deng Gai, who had sufficiently represented the president." See: Craig, "Analysts: Absence of South Sudan President from IGAD Summit Problematic."

such as churches and ethnic groups, in brokering local peace agreements, and urged, "IGAD and the region could consider ways to help to ensure these constituencies are represented at the table. I commend the work of the churches in thinking creatively how to bring people together."[43]

Later that year, IGAD, together with the AU, and other partners such as the UN and the Troika, established a High-Level Revitalization Forum (HLRF). The renewed efforts to resolve the dead-end in South Sudan included expanding the circle of parties to add, in addition to high-rank politicians, various South Sudanese stakeholders, such as representatives of civil society groups (such as elders, women and youth), and even representatives of non-state armed groups and informal pastoralist armies.[44] However, as was the case in 2013, the 2015 efforts to integrate civil society groups into the conflict resolution efforts stemmed from a combination of the political elites' lack of commitment of a truly inclusive process, and the divisions among the civil society groups themselves, which struggled to find a common denominator among themselves.[45]

The High Level Revitalization Forum was launched on December 18, 2017. The official IGAD document noticed that:

> The High Level Revitalization Forum concluded its first phase today with the signing of an Agreement on Cessation of Hostilities, Protection of Civilians and Humanitarian Access. The IGAD Special Envoy for South Sudan Ambassador Ismail Wais and the Co-Facilitators of the Forum H.E. Ramtane Lamamra, H.E. Hanna Tetteh and H.E. George Rebello Chicoti announced the successful conclusion of the first phase of the High Level Revitalization Forum. They expressed their appreciation to the South Sudanese stakeholders, representatives of the government, opposition parties, armed and non-armed groups as well as the representatives of civil society organizations, eminent persons, business, women and youth for the success they achieved. They also congratulated the stakeholders for their commitment in the revitalization process as demonstrated by the constructive manner, in which they participated in the discussions that allowed for the conclusion of an agreement. The Cessation of Hostilities Agreement shall come into force at 00:01 hours (South Sudan local time)

43 IGAD, "Briefing to the IGAD Extraordinary Summit on the Situation in South Sudan by United Nations Special Representative of the Secretary-General David Shearer," June 12, 2017.

44 Wild, Jok, and Pate, "The Militarization of Cattle Raiding in South Sudan," 8.

45 Tanza, "South Sudan Warring Parties Ink a Cease-Fire Deal."

> on the 24th December 2017. The Agreement sets the stage for further discussions, required for the Revitalization Process.[46]

Indeed, a month later, a two-day meeting was convened by IGAD's South Sudan office in Bishoftu, Ethiopia. The meeting was attended by 22 participants – politicians, academic scholars, representatives of civil society organizations, and representatives of IGAD (including JMEC), AU, UN, and the EU. The official purpose of the meeting was to engage in a frank dialogue and develop recommendations on the continuation of the revitalization process.[47]

Does the HLRF mark a change in IGAD's mediation strategy? Some analysts are already claiming that IGAD failed to address specific questions about objectives and timetables, and failed to draw lessons from the failures of previous agreements.[48] While Festus Mogae, Chairperson of JMEC, may have sought to draw lessons from the failures of the ARCSS and called for the "revitalization process [to] address the current political realities in South Sudan … and seek ways in which key actors can be identified and engaged or re-engaged,"[49] it seemed that many of the crucial issues were left unresolved. One of these crucial issues was the upcoming expiry in July 2018 of the mandate of South Sudan's transitional government, and subsequent elections. No discussion of this issue took place, in order to prevent aggravating tensions in an already fragile situation. Jacob Dut Chol, professor of politics at Juba University, claimed that: "There are very strong caveat to these things of elections, you must ensure there is peace, ceasefire in the country. To do elections you need voters in Upper Nile, Equatoria regions, and genuine peace not just peace you hear in newspapers, but peace that shows there are no gunshots."[50] More recently, IGAD suspended the South Sudan revitalization talks when a large number of opposition groups demanded that Kiir be excluded from the transitional government, a demand that was obviously rejected by Juba.[51]

Another issue that showed no signs of improvement was the fate of the contested regions (mainly the Blue Nile, South Kordofan, Abyei, and to some extent, Darfur) that had been excluded from the CPA. The remainder of this

46 IGAD, "High level Revitalization Forum for the Resolution of the Conflict in South Sudan Concluded with Signing of an Agreement on Cessation of Hostilities," December 18, 2017.

47 EU, "Joint Press Release by the EU and IGAD on the Informal Ministerial Meeting with Foreign Ministers from Member Countries."

48 Soliman and Verjee, "How to Support South Sudan's High Level Revitalization Forum."

49 Quoted in *ibid.*, 2.

50 Quoted in: Elamu, "News Analysis: South Sudan May Miss 2018 Elections."

51 "IGAD Suspends South Sudan Peace Revitalization Talks," February 17, 2018.

chapter examines the developments in the contested regions since South Sudan's independence and analyzes IGAD's current role there.

As mentioned in previous chapters, South Kordofan, the Blue Nile, and Abeyi were excluded from the arrangement that allowed the South Sudanese to vote for secession in January 2011. While Blue Nile and South Kordofan were not granted similar right to a referendum on their independence, the CPA granted the two states the right to "popular consultation," a vaguely defined mechanism designed to ascertain the views of the states' populations on whether the CPA had fulfilled their aspirations. In the case of South Kordofan, the popular consultation was constantly delayed as state elections were postponed. In Blue Nile, however, a Popular Consultation Commission was established. As the process of popular consultation gained momentum and the possibility that the region's inhabitants would choose self-rule (*al-hukmal-zati*) increased, Khartoum became alarmed, and NCP politicians blamed local leaders of promoting secessionism, in an attempt to follow South Sudan.[52] In effect, de Waal claims that the fate of the "regions" served as a political tool for both parties of the CPA:

> Separation did not resolve the political competition between Khartoum and Juba. As part of that competition, South Sudan sponsored the SPLM/A-North in a full-blown insurrection in the 'Two Areas' of southern Kordofan and the Blue Nile, where the SPLM had strong constituencies, including two capable army divisions. Khartoum's political-business managers made a characteristic miscalculation: they were confident that, if they could humble Juba and buy off a sufficient quota of the local elites in the 'Two Areas,' they would resolve the problem. They were wrong.[53]

One month after South Sudan's independence, war broke out between the Sudanese government and the SPLM-N in South Kordofan State, and many realized that it was a matter of time before the violence spread to Blue Nile as well. Indeed, on the night of September 1, 2011, fighting broke out once more in Blue Nile State. As was the case in South Sudan, civil war in those areas led to a continued humanitarian crisis that included wide-scale personal and communal insecurity and food insecurity. Displacement also was one of the features of the humanitarian crisis. Displacement figures in 2016, for example, show that 172,000 people fled Blue Nile State to South Sudan and Ethiopia, and a similar number of people had been displaced within Sudan. In total, these numbers

52 Carter Center, "Carter Center Urges Political Parties and Blue Nile Popular Consultation Commission to Ensure Genuine Dialogue on Key Issues in Blue Nile State."

53 de Waal, *The Real Politics of the Horn of Africa*, 88.

amount to some 40% of the state's population. Since then, fighting and peace negotiations continued simultaneously.[54] In 2016, for example, Khartoum and several rebel factions signed the African Union High Level Implementation Panel (AUHIP) Roadmap Agreement to end the conflicts in Darfur, Blue Nile, and South Kordofan. A mere several months later, both parties violated the agreement and violence erupted once again in South Kordofan.[55]

The fate of the "two areas" was recently discussed in the 2017 Human Rights Watch report, which blamed the Sudanese government for the continuing violence in Darfur, Southern Kordofan, and Blue Nile, and its use of Sudan's Rapid Support Forces (RSF) and other government-aligned forces to attack civilians. It also blamed Sudan for failing to provide accountability for serious crimes committed during the conflicts, or serious human rights violations:

> In Southern Kordofan and Blue Nile, the six-year conflict continued, with sporadic government attacks on civilians. In Blue Nile and in refugee camps in neighboring South Sudan, displaced communities fought along ethnic lines following a split within the leadership of the armed opposition, Sudan People's Liberation Army-North. In the rebel held areas of both states, hundreds of thousands lacked sufficient food and basic supplies because the government and rebels failed to agree on modalities for the delivery of essential items. In Southern Kordofan and Blue Nile, the six-year conflict continued, with sporadic government attacks on civilians. In Blue Nile and in refugee camps in neighboring South Sudan, displaced communities fought along ethnic lines following a split within the leadership of the armed opposition, Sudan People's Liberation Army-North. In the rebel held areas of both states, hundreds of thousands lacked sufficient food and basic supplies because the government and rebels failed to agree on modalities for the delivery of essential items.[56]

Moreover, as was the case in the civil war in South Sudan, the local groups in the region were becoming increasingly splintered as the war continued. Recently, for example, the SPLM-N divided into two factions: one in the Nuba Mountains led by Abdel Aziz al-Hilu and the other in the White Nile State led by Malik Agar. The split, which occurred over various issues including the right

54 Gidron, "Five Years of War in Blue Nile State: Hope and Despair between the Two Sudans," 6.
55 Genser, "The United Nations Security Council's Implementation of the Responsibility to Protect," 465.
56 For the full report, see: Human Rights Watch, "Sudan: Events of 2017." See also Gesner, who claims that: "The Office of the High Commissioner for Human Rights released a report on the situation of human rights in Sudan in August 2011 listing atrocities committed by the SAF, stating these likely constitute war crimes and crimes against humanity," *ibid.*, 466.

of self-determination, further hampers IGAD's mediation efforts.[57] As a result, "mediators met the two factions last August, but they didn't fix a clear position on the matter, while the facilitators from the Troika countries and the European Union also didn't determine a unified position on the matter."[58] Another meeting, in September 2017 between Lesane Johannes, representative of the IGAD in Khartoum and Sudan's Presidential Assistant Ibrahim Mahmoud, who met to discuss arrangements to resume Sudan's peace talks on the Two Areas, ended without significant results.

Although the conflicts in all three contested regions hinged on issues of self-determination and belonging, the situation in Abyei differed due to its oil resources. The contested status of oil-rich Abyei was an obstacle to the progress of the CPA negotiations, and was never resolved. This fact caused damage not only to South Sudan's failing economy, but also caused considerable difficulties to Sudan's economy, which had been crippled by its loss of oil revenues after the succession of South Sudan in 2011. Sudan's declaration of a new budget in January 2018 included devaluation of the Sudanese pound against the dollar, a move that triggered inflation and rising prices of bread and other basic foodstuffs, and sparked a wave of protests across the country.[59] The deteriorating economic situation in both countries motivated their leaders to find an escape from the stalemate. An official Ethiopian publication described the atmosphere:

> After talks last week, South Sudan and Sudan agreed to resume production from the oil field in the Unity region. South Sudan Ambassador to Sudan, Mayan Dut Waal, said at the weekend that Sudan would provide power and technical support to resume production, stopped since December 2013. He said the security situation in the region was now stable and expressed the hope this would increase South Sudan's oil production to over 300,000 bpd instead of the current production rate of 130,000 bpd. South Sudan announced on Wednesday (October 4) that it was holding discussions with Sudan over utilizing water transport in order to boost

57 For a detailed analysis of the reasons for the split, see: Young, "SPLM-NORTH: What Went Wrong?."

58 *Sudan Tribune*, "Sudan, IGAD Discuss Resumption of Two Areas Peace Talks."

59 The violent reactions of the police toward the protesters (that in general protested in a peaceful manner) and the arrests of hundreds of them, including several opposition leaders, sparked once again the criticism against the dubious reputation of Sudan as a constant violator of human rights. It should be remembered that the two arrest warrants against al-Bashir are still legally valid, and the issue regarding his visits in IGAD countries is still under discussion. See, for example: *Daily Nation*, "Court Lifts President al-Bashir Arrest Warrant."

> trade between the two countries. Trade minister, Moses Hassan Tiel, said the Nile was the main trade route between Juba and Khartoum and reopening river transport with Sudan would reduce the cost of doing business. River transport was halted in 2012.[60]

Yet, despite the mutual recognition of the need to reconstruct the oil industry for the benefit of the economies of both countries, and the understanding that a decision regarding the fate of Abyei region is a crucial step toward reconstruction, the issue remains unresolved. Moreover, during Kiir's last visit in Khartoum it was clearly declared that there would be no discussion of the issue of Abyei. Although one of his speakers praised the IGAD-initiated revitalization program, and said that that his government is looking forward to its implementation, he declared that, "The agenda of the issues to be discussed has been finalized and unless it is revised before the president travel, I don't think the issue of Abyei will be a subject of discussion because it is not one of the talking points based on the content of the current agenda."[61]

In retrospect, the reasons for the fact the IGAD-mediated agreements and mechanisms left numerous disputed issues unresolved are perhaps based on the belief that these issues would eventually be resolved through negotiations between the rival factions. This assumption proved to be problematic, for example regarding the fate of the contested regions, an issue that remains unsettled thirteen years after the signing of the CPA, and almost seven years after its implementation. Additional issues that could not have been predicted at the time, such as the outbreak of the civil war in South Sudan,[62] demanded new, intensive mediation efforts that have so far failed to bear fruit. To further evaluate the contribution of IGAD's mediation at the regional level, the next and final chapter compares IGAD's involvement in South Sudan to its involvement in Somalia, where IGAD's role had deep roots.

---

60 Federal Democratic Republic of Ethiopia, "A Week in the Horn," 15.

61 *Sudan Tribune*, "South Sudan President Will Not Discuss Abyei in Khartoum."

62 Back, "IGAD, Sudan and South Sudan: Achievements and Setbacks of Regional Mediation."

CHAPTER 6

A Comparative View of IGAD's Mediation in Sudan, Somalia, South Sudan, and Somaliland

At the turn of the century, the IGAD region faced extremely turbulent times. The fragility of the situation in this region was described by the US ambassador in Kenya at the time, Johnnie Carson:

> The collapse of the Somali state, more than 15 years of civil war in the Sudan, the on-going conflict between the Lord Resistance Army and the Ugandan authorities, the unfortunate (but hopefully now concluded) war between Ethiopia and Eritrea, have combined to cause enormous destruction and have set back economic development in the IGAD area. These conflicts have increased the flow of arms in the region, created an enormous refugee crisis, increased tension and instability along borders and created a political climate that says open conflict is acceptable to resolve problems.[1]

Carson's choice to mention Somalia and Sudan first was not coincidental. The ongoing crises in these two countries threatened the stability of the entire region.

This chapter reviews IGAD's mediation efforts in Somalia, which are then compared to its mediation efforts in the cases of Sudan and South Sudan, focusing on three main questions: First, what were the differences in IGAD's mediation patterns between Sudan (a state with a relatively centralized political center) and Somalia (a state with a weak and decentralized political center)?[2] Second, what were the differences between IGAD's reliance on international, continental, and regional assistance in its mediation efforts in these two cases? The third question, on issues of state sovereignty and intervention, demands a more complex exploration, and focuses on IGAD's attitudes toward separatists' aspirations in South Sudan and in Somaliland (a region in Somalia).

1 Johnnie Carson's address to the first CEWRAN meeting, Nairobi, 5 July 2000, quoted in Juma, "The Intergovernmental Authority on Development and the East African Community," 229.

2 Murithi, "Inter-governmental Authority on Development on the Ground: Comparing Interventions in Sudan and Somalia."

 | DOI:10.1163/9789004425323_008

One of the emphases of IGAD's mediation efforts was the issue of its inclusiveness. In effect, the Somali negotiation process was arguably much more inclusive than the Sudanese and South Sudanese processes, and included many representatives from different strata of Somali society from an early stage. Although it could be claimed that levels of inclusiveness stemmed from the different political features and structure of the two states (centralized vs. decentralized, etc.), it was often argued (and shown in the previous chapters) that the Sudanese peace process was very elitist in nature, paying only lip service to mass participation in it. This chapter offers an in-depth analysis of this argument, and a review of its strength and weakness.

This chapter focuses on IGAD's mediation in the civil war that erupted in 1991,[3] whose scale and severity made Somalia the prime example of what Robert Rotberg has termed a "collapsed state": "A rare and extreme version of the failed state" that is "a mere geographical expression, a black hole into which a failed polity has fallen," where "there is dark energy, but the forces of entropy have overwhelmed the radiance that hitherto provided some semblance of order and other vital political goods to the inhabitants (no longer the citizens) embraced by language or ethnic affinities or borders."[4]

Contrary to Sudan, Somalia did not have a history of internal divisions or civil war after its independence, yet its problematic colonial heritage (discussed below) and the effects of Siad Barre's dictatorial regime (1969–1991) established the grounds for Somalia's dysfunctional political center. According to Menkhaus, these features were prevalent before the collapse of Barre's regime in 1991:

> Ample evidence suggests that by the mid-1980s Somalia was already a failed state. With the partial exception of the security sector, most government institutions began to atrophy in the years following the disastrous Ogaden War with Ethiopia in 1977–78. Fierce government repression, heightened clan cleavages and animosities, gross levels of corruption, and low salaries all combined to accelerate the state's decline.[5]

3 The events that led to the outbreak of the Somali's civil war in 1991 have been described at length elsewhere. See, for example: Lewis, *Making and Breaking States in Africa: The Somali Experience*; Brons, *Society, Security, Sovereignty and the State in Somalia: From Statelessness to Statelessness?*.

4 Quoted in Pham, "State Collapse, Insurgency, and Famine in the Horn of Africa," 154.

5 Menkhaus, "Governance without Government in Somalia: Spoilers, State Building, and the Politics of Coping," 83. See also: Erlich, *Islam and Christianity in the Horn of Africa: Somalia, Ethiopia and Sudan*.

Therefore, while mediation efforts in Sudan the early 1990s were mainly focused on efforts to promote peace agreements, efforts in Somalia in the same period were first concentrated to block the spread of violence and prevent famine.[6] After intensive diplomatic efforts by both the UN and the OAU the country's two key factions signed a ceasefire agreement in March 1992. With the understanding that some kind of peacekeeping force would be required to sustain the agreement and ensure humanitarian relief efforts, the Security Council adopted Resolution 751, which led to the establishment of United Nations Operation in Somalia (UNOSOM), a monitoring force.[7] However, the rival parties' general contempt for the ceasefire agreement and the deteriorating humanitarian conditions motivated the US government to lead a Unified Task Force (UNITAF) under UN auspices, for a five-month period, which became known as Operation Restore Hope.

The new force (later transformed into UNOSOM II by Security Council Recommendation 837 of March 1993)[8] was assigned to develop a model for task-sharing between the UN and the US government, and its establishment was followed by overly optimistic expectations that it would establish a new model for peacekeeping and reconstruction of a "collapsed state." With 28,000 personnel from 26 countries and an annual budget of US$ 1.6 billion, UNOSOM II was expected to establish a new transitional government, supervise the disarmament of the forces, reconstruct the infrastructures, and resettle refugees. However, events of July–October 1993 were changing the situation completely, in the sense that they determined not only the fate of Operation Restore Hope, but also the fate of future international interventions in intrastate African conflicts.

In June 1993, 24 Pakistani UNOSOM troops were killed in an ambush by a Somali militia allegedly belonging to one of the powerful warlords, General Mohamed Farah Aidid. Following this incident, most UNOSOM efforts were redirected to defeating Aidid's forces and personally capturing him. These efforts included a combined aerial and ground attack on July 12 on a house that was believed to be hosting a meeting of members of his movement, whom the Americans suspected were planning additional attacks against US and UN forces. Growing tensions between Aidid's factions and the international force led to the Battle of Mogadishu on October 3–4, where two US Black Hawk helicopters were shot down, 18 American soldiers were killed, and 73 wounded. Although the Somali casualties significantly outnumbered American casualties, the images of the failed American operation, and especially

6 Woodward, "Somalia and Sudan: A Tale of Two Peace Processes," 472.
7 "Somalia – UNOSOM I" (1992).
8 "Somalia – UNOSOM II" (1993).

the images of the bodies of two US soldiers being dragged through the streets, had a tremendous impact on American and Western public opinion regarding intervention in risky areas overseas.[9] When the US government decided to withdraw its forces from Somalia shortly thereafter, other nations followed suit, and UNOSOM was finally disbanded in March 1995. The failure of Restore Hope Operation and the withdrawal of the US and UN forces from Somalia, deterred further initiatives based on direct international intervention in Somalia. In the wider context of Africa, this created expectations that regional organizations, including IGAD, would take the place of international organizations. Indeed, between 1991 and 1997, IGAD made thirteen attempts to institute a functioning government and reestablish the state of Somalia. The attempts were futile, on all occasions.[10] Notably, the failure of this operation also played an important role in the international community's increased reluctance to intervene in the future in intrastate conflicts that place peacekeeping forces in life-threatening situations.

While the eyes of the international community had been turned to the events that followed the American and UN intervention,[11] intervention in Somalia by the regional African organization drew almost no international attention. Kinfe Abraham, an Ethiopian scholar who also served as the director-general for Political and Humanitarian Affairs before serving as the acting deputy executive secretary of IGAD, described the ongoing regional efforts to resolve the Somali debacle that were already evident soon after the outbreak of the conflict. He reviewed two conferences held in Djibouti in 1991 that were aimed to promote national reconciliation. IGAD was involved in the second conference, and two of its leaders, the presidents of Kenya and Uganda, were actively involved in the efforts to reach a solution.[12]

It seemed that already in that early stage, the seeds of a recurrent pattern of failure in mediations between the rival parties were sown by the exclusion of groups considered radical, as Mulugeta describes:

> The participants agreed to hold a national reconciliation conference. Accordingly, the government of Djibouti convened the second conference in July, 1991. At the end of the meeting, the Somali participants agreed to

9 Hirsh and Oakley, *Somalia and Operation Restore Hope: Reflections on Peacemaking and Peacekeeping*. Public images of the events of this battle were also influenced by the popular movie *Black Hawk Down*, directed by Ridley Scott in 2001.

10 Abraham explained that: "This made the burden of countries like Ethiopia, with the Mandate of IGAD and the OAU, in trying to bring peace to Somalia so much more difficult."

11 See, for example: Prunier, "Somalia: Civil War, Intervention and Withdrawal."

12 Abraham, *Somalia Calling: The Crisis of Statehood and the Quest for Peace*, 65–6.

> a cease-fire and to establish a provisional government. However, the agreement did not hold. One of the powerful faction leaders, General Aidid rejected the new government, which resulted in widespread violence. The SNM, which declared the independence of Somaliland, also boycotted the meeting.[13]

A glimmer of hope for a breakthrough in the negotiation process emerged in late October 1996, when a mandate was given both to IGAD and the OAU to assemble representatives of 26 Somali factions, first in Addis Ababa and then in Sodere. This second convention resulted in Sodere Declaration, which included agreements on issues such as establishing a joint municipal police force and reopening the Mogadishu seaport and airport. The Declaration was applauded by many international, continental, and regional actors, and backed by the financial support of many donors including the OAU and the IGAD Partner Forum (IPF), yet its implementation was undermined, once again, by the exclusion of several Somali factions, such as the faction of the powerful leader Muhammad Aidid.[14]

Another potential breakthrough in the negotiation process emerged at the Somali National Peace Conference, which was held in Arta, Djibouti, between 1999 and 2000. This conference was attended by 1,200 delegates from all walks of Somali society, including elders, religious leaders, women, and intellectuals, as well as approximately 1,500 external observers. The IGAD-led Somali Peace Conference held in Arta was the longest initiative ever held to resolve the Somalia crisis, and its scope extended to issues such as arms control, disarmament of the militia, looted property, and the status of Mogadishu. Moreover, following five months of deliberations after the Arta Conference, the establishment Transitional National Government (TNG) was declared.[15] Hopes that this round of negotiations would be a breakthrough in ongoing civil war in Somalia were voiced by Ismael Omar Guelleh, president of Djibouti, in his address to the Eighth IGAD Summit of Heads of State and Government:

> Arta, he said, was simply the culmination of a long and tortuous process that began a decade earlier in Djibouti, and involved thereafter many

13 Mulugeta, "The Role of Regional and International Organizations in Resolving the Somali Conflict: The Case of IGAD," 26.

14 For a detailed description of the Sodere process and outcomes, including its documentation, see: Abraham, *Somalia Calling: The Crisis of Statehood and the Quest for Peace*, 129–248.

15 Juma, "The Intergovernmental Authority on Development and the East African Community," 237.

> players and countries particularly: IGAD countries, the United Nations, the OAU, the League of Arab States and the OIC. Arta succeeded because it was a bottom-up approach to conflict resolution involving all the stakeholders, he said. He added that its success depended also on the extreme sacrifices the people of Djibouti made in giving material and moral support for the people of Somalia given the meagre [sic] resources at their disposal.[16]

Yet, it soon became clear that the outcome of the Arta Conference decisions was not fundamentally different from those of the previous conferences. Like the previous rounds of negotiations, the Arta Peace Conference became a sphere of competing individual political interests rather than an attempt to find a comprehensive solution to the country's situation. In this context, Kenneth Menkhaus noted, "Nearly all energy invested in the Arta process (which culminated in the creation of the TNG) focused on the division of anticipated spoils; namely, the share of seats in the parliament and cabinet by clan ... the TNG was in essence a piece of paper on a fish hook, thrown into international waters to lure foreign aid which could then be diverted into appropriate pockets."[17] Ghirmazion argued that "The Arta Peace Process moved the old politicians and the traditional leaders closer and has empowered one group of the politicians. The IGAD-led Somali Peace Conference gave some sort of legitimacy to the new politicians and since then politics of exclusion has been applied including cabinet appointments that were limited to the sitting lawmakers."[18]

Yet, the fate of the negotiations concerning the ongoing Somali crisis was also to be determined by the September 11, 2001 terror attack in the United States, which changed the course of global events at the turn of the millennium. Arguably, September 11 affected Somalia's definition as a central site to implement the new conception of the "War on terror" and its marginalization within the new international order. These consequences ultimately led to an escalation in internal fragmentation, which further complicated mediation efforts. Yet, these consequences were revealed only much later, and could not be predicted in 2002–2004, when mediation efforts in Somalia (including by IGAD) resumed.

---

16 Khartoum Declaration of IGAD Eighth Summit of Heads of State and Government, Khartoum.

17 Menkhaus, "State Collapse in Somalia: Second Thoughts," 419.

18 Ghirmazion, "In Quest for a Culture of Peace in the IGAD Region: The Role of Intellectuals and Scholars," 183.

One of the main reasons for the renewed hopes was the involvement in the Somali mediation process of Kenya, which was already considered a highly skilled regional mediator. It was Kenya's President Daniel Arap Moi who announced a plan for a full national reconciliation conference to be convened at Eldoret, Kenya, and in September 2002 a proposed framework for the Somali National Reconciliation Process was presented to the IGAD Council of Ministers. The Eldoret process (known also as the Mbagathi Process) involved several hundred Somali political, military, traditional, and civil society notables that were supposed to agree on desired outcomes of the peace process, determine the core issues to be addressed, and agree to a cessation of hostilities. The process was supposed to be led by IGAD's technical committee of the "Frontline States" (Djibouti, Ethiopia, and Kenya) under Kenyan chairmanship, who suggested that the complex and comprehensive dialogue would require at least six to nine months.

Moreover, it seemed that under the new leadership of Kenya, which was considered an important ally of the West, former hesitations regarding a deeper commitment by the broader international community were reconsidered. At this stage, following Kenya's dominance in the Somali mediation process and the renewed international involvement, it seemed that the negotiation process *could* make unprecedented progress.[19]

At first, the Eldoret dialogue seemed to be based on a comprehensive framework, as most major political movements (with the exception of the self-declared Republic of Somaliland in the northwest of the country, which is described below) were represented, and key members of the international community closely monitored each step. However, as the process progressed, several major shortcomings were revealed. Some of those setbacks were external, such as rivalries between regional powers or the sustained international readiness to adopt and implement targeted sanctions against recalcitrant warlords and enforce an international arms embargo.[20] Other setbacks were related to internal Somali politics, such as the fact that the talks were repeatedly interrupted by violations of the weakly drafted "ceasefire." Moreover, although the peace process involved political leaders, military leaders, and traditional elders, it was unable to devise a formula that would deal effectively with issues such as power-sharing between warlords, as described by Pham:

---

19 See International Crisis Group, "Ending Starvation as a Weapon of War in Sudan," and "Salvaging Somalia's Chance for Peace."

20 For the historical analysis of what is termed "warlords" in Somalia, see: Abbink, "Dervishes, 'Moryaan' and Freedom Fighters: Cycles of Rebellion and the Fragmentation of Somali Society, 1900–2000."

> The discussions were so protracted that it took just over two years to establish the TFG using the "4.5 formula." According to this framework, power was to be shared between four of the clan-families – Darod, Dir, Hawiye, and Digil Mirifle (the Isaq, centered in Somaliland, declined to participate) – with some space (the "0.5") granted to minority clans. The Transitional Federal Charter agreed to in October 2004 gave the Transitional Federal Institutions of government a five-year mandate. Heading up this structure was a Darod warlord, Abdullahi Yusuf Ahmad, who had launched his national political career with the proceeds of a $1 million ransom he had extracted from the Taiwanese after his militia seized the trawler MV Shen Kno II in 1997.[21]

After two years of IGAD-sponsored peace talks between various Somali clans and factions, and despite the challenges of the mediation process, a breakthrough occurred in August 2004 when the parties selected the parliamentarians of the transitional government in Somalia. In clear contrast to the Arta process, the Transitional Federal Charter proposed a federal structure for the state and defined the transitional tasks of the government and its institutions. From the inauguration of the country's Transitional Federal Government (TFG), which was formed in Kenya in December 2004, the TFG won immediate international recognition. Substantial financial support was also anticipated with the inauguration of a World Bank and UNDP Joint Needs Assessment of the country's rehabilitation and development requirements. Nonetheless, like its predecessor, the TFG fell well short of serving as a national government. Instead, power was concentrated in a narrow clan coalition, and in Somalia the TFG was viewed as a client of Ethiopia. A Mogadishu-based coalition, comprising dominant clans from the capital, Islamists, leaders of the previous TNG, and warlords, formed an opposition to the TFG and blocked it from establishing itself in the capital.

In light of these developments, IGAD's involvement in Somalia resumed in September 2006, when the AU endorsed the IGAD Peace Support Mission in Somalia (IGASOM) to support the TFG's relocation to Mogadishu from Nairobi.[22] IGASOM, however, proved to be an ineffective organ and failed to lead a process of national reconciliation and control of the country. Feelings of despair and hopelessness were prevalent among many Somalis, as Ghirmazion described:

21 Pham, "State Collapse, Insurgency, and Famine in the Horn of Africa: Legitimacy and the Ongoing Somali Crisis," 162–3.

22 IRIN, "IGAD to Deploy Peacekeepers Despite Opposition by Faction Leaders."

> In present-day Somalia, criminal offences and human rights abuses are the order of the day with its perpetrators enjoying unlimited freedom. Trade in arms is a booming business with automatic assault rifles easily available for sale throughout the country. The unregulated arms proliferation and trafficking is threatening the stability of the entire Horn of Africa region. The president of the TFG has repeatedly called for lifting of the arms embargo to Somalia to allow performance in the field of security. His rivals both within the government and outside vehemently opposed the appeal and instead urged the international community and in particular the UN Security Council to maintain the arms embargo. They further argued that measures to disarm and collect the abundant arms in Somalia are required rather than marketing new consignments, which would only exacerbate the already fluid situation.[23]

This prevalence of violence and insecurity may explain why Mogadishu was rather easily seized by the Islamic Courts Union (ICU) – a coalition of local shari'a courts and Islamists – in June 2006.[24] Although the Islamists' short period of rule in Somalia was considered a period of relative stability, unknown in Somalia since 1991, the ICU's victory triggered apprehension in and outside Somalia. The ICU-led coalition, which contained both moderate and extremist factions, also contained a faction named Harakat al-Shabaab al Mujaahidiin ("the Youth Movement of the Jihadists," better-known as al-Shabaab), which was the best-trained, best-equipped, and most strongly committed faction in the coalition, and attracted the most concerns. Ideologically, al-Shabaab follows the doctrine of *takfiri*, which allows its members to declare other Muslims unbelievers (*kafir*), resist foreign presence on their land (including peacekeepers; a fact that had major importance for the future AU peacekeeping force), and commit suicide to kill their enemy.[25] Al-Shabaab was also subsequently suspected of ties with al-Qaeda.[26]

Both the West and neighboring Ethiopia became increasingly alarmed in the face of the growing dominance of radical Islam in Somalia, and Ethiopian

23 Ghirmazion, *In Quest for a Culture of Peace in the IGAD Region: The Role of Intellectuals and Scholars*, 171.

24 They were defeating the Alliance for the Restoration of Peace and Counter-Terrorism there.

25 Ingiriis, "Building Peace from the Margins in Somalia: The Case for Political Settlement with Al-Shabaab," 4–10.

26 ICU alignment with al-Qaeda was confirmed in February 2010. See: Botha, "Who's Who in the Somali Quagmire?"

troops hastened to invade Somalia in December 2006 in response to the call of Somalia's TFG President Abdullahi Yusuf. The TFG president's call for outside military intervention turned out to be very unpopular in the eyes of many segments of Somali society, and ignited a new wave of internal violence throughout the country. Although Ethiopia announced that it would not remain in Somalia after the defeat of the ICU, and would withdraw as soon as a peacekeeping operation stabilized the situation sufficiently, Ethiopian presence aggravated domestic violence even further. Ethiopian troops' invasion to Mogadishu, after ICU assumed control of the city, not only triggered a new wave of internal violence throughout the country[27] but also illuminated some of the main shortcomings of regional mediation that were manifest on several levels.

First, besides the highly contentious issue of the military invasion by one IGAD member state of another member state, the fragility of IGAD's authority to mediate in the Somali conflict was also revealed by the fact that Eritrea suspended its membership in IGAD, which was one of several indications of the declining support for the organization's operations and its ineffective handling of the complicated dynamics of regional relationships.[28] Second, as mentioned, although they were originally designed to be inclusive and represent all walks of Somali society, the IGAD-mediated talks effectively excluded many groups from various stages of the mediation process, due to member states' opposition to the inclusion of Islamist groups, and not even necessarily radical ones. Kidist Mulugeta referred to both issues:

> Ethiopia also managed to successfully galvanize the endorsement of all IGAD members – except Eritrea – for its intervention in Somalia. IGAD's support to the Ethiopian intervention had faced strong opposition from Eritrea, which claimed that IGAD is partial to Ethiopia and the US… There were a number of Islamist movements during the Eldoret peace conference that were actively involved in the provision of social services. However, the Eldoret peace process denied them any place and role. This is due to the lack of comfort from the members of IGAD, particularly Kenya, Ethiopia, and Uganda. The so-called moderate Islamist groups

27 During 2007 alone, fighting between the TFG and the insurgency caused the deaths of several thousand civilians, the displacement of up to 700,000 people from Mogadishu, and widespread destruction of the city.

28 Mulugeta, "The Role of Regional and International Organizations in Resolving the Somali Conflict: The Case of IGAD." See also: Andemariam, "In, Out or at the Gate? The Predicament on Eritrea's Membership and Participation Status in IGAD."

were recognized and represented for the first time during the Djibouti peace process, organized under the auspicious of the UN.[29]

In response to a UN call to bolster IGAD's status and intervene in the escalating Somali conflict, a small contingent of African Union peacekeepers was deployed to Mogadishu in early 2007. The African Union Mission in Somalia (AMISOM) was created by the PSC on January 19, 2007, with an initial six-month mandate.[30] The following month, Security Council Resolution 1744 approved the mission's mandate, which included support for TFI's (Transitional Federal Institutions) efforts to stabilize the country; promote dialogue and reconciliation; facilitate humanitarian assistance; and create favorable conditions for long-term stabilization, reconstruction, and development in Somalia.[31]

The year 2008 was a year of escalated efforts to find a solution to the deteriorating situation in Somalia, which had become the worst humanitarian and political crisis the country experienced since the early 1990s.[32] Both the UN and IGAD were involved in these efforts. A further round of mediation efforts was initiated by the UN to end the fighting between the TFG and proliferation of armed opposition forces. In May 2008, IGAD-led peace talks under the auspices of the UN began in Djibouti between the Alliance for the Re-Liberation of Somalia (ARS)–Djibouti faction and the TFG. After several rounds of negotiations and signed agreements, new elections for the transitional federal presidency were held in Djibouti in early 2009. The election of Sheikh Sharif Sheikh Ahmed as the new TFG president marked the conclusion of the fourteenth IGAD-led Somalia peace and reconciliation negotiation process. Yet, once again, by including only the moderate Islamist wing and excluding the radical wing, this agreement created the potential for further conflicts.[33]

Moreover, on the ground, the ongoing conflict, combined with ecological factors such as the continuing drought, led to the outbreak of a severe famine

---

29 *Ibid.*, 40, 43.

30 Hull and Svensson, *African Union Mission in Somalia (AMISOM): Exemplifying African Union Peacekeeping Challenges.*

31 AU Peace and Security Council (Somalia) Communiqué, PSC/PR/Comm. (LXIX); Healy "IGAD and Regional Security in the Horn."

32 Menkhaus, Sheikh, Joqombe, and Johnson, "The Search for Peace, Somali Programme: A History of Mediation in Somalia since 1988."

33 UIC's military defeat in January 2007 led to a fragmentation between two distinct factions, a moderate and a radical one. The Alliance for the Re-liberation of Somalia (ARS), led by Sharif Sheikh Ahmed, was incorporated into the transitional government through the Djibouti peace deal (Power-Sharing), signed in 2008, and al-Shabaab, led by Sheikh Hassan Dahir Aweyis, became the main challenge to the consolidation of peace in Somalia. See: Cardoso, "Regional Security in the Horn of Africa: Conflicts, Agendas and Threats," 137.

in 2011–12, in which nearly 260,000 people, mostly children, died of hunger and disease. According to *The Guardian*:

> The drought, the worst in the region for 60 years, led to livestock deaths, reduced harvests, and drops in labour demand and household incomes. Poor harvests drove food prices to extreme levels, said the report. The situation was compounded by conflict and insecurity in Somalia, which impeded the delivery of food aid. The Islamist group al-Shabaab was at war with the government, and areas the group controlled were some of those worst affected by the crisis.[34]

As this article mentions, the humanitarian crisis in Somalia was closely interwoven with a general deterioration of the security situation, which became even worse in the following years. In October 2011, following terror attacks by al-Shabaab within Kenya, it launched Operation Linda Nchi (Kiswahili for "Protect the Nation") and has since deployed a 4000-strong force in Somalia, between their common border and the port town of Kismayu, including both ground and air units, which aimed to combat Islamic radicalism within Somalia, and aimed to restore regional stability and development. The Kenyan invasion sparked another wave of terror attacks, including the well-known assault on the Westgate Mall at the outskirt of Nairobi, which claimed the lives of at least 72 persons and injured over 200 people, renewing the threat to regional stability.[35] In response, Ambassador Mahboub Maalim, IGAD executive secretary at the time, reiterated the organization's commitments, stating, "Let it be known that these terrorists shall neither discourage IGAD and the Member States in their collective efforts in Somalia nor intimidate AMISOM forces into pulling out of Somalia until total peace and stability has been achieved."[36]

Later that year, Maalim outlined a Six Pillar Priority Program for Somalia that "outlines the Somali government's main priority areas for development, and has been subsumed into the IGAD Regional Grand Stabilization Plan; the Somali government's 2016 Vision for Somalia, which outlines the process for creating a Somali federal system, removing al-Shabaab, and holding elections in 2016; and the December 2012 Addis Ababa agreement, which promotes

34 *The Guardian*, "Somalia Famine in 2010–12 Worst in Past 25 Years."
35 Back, "Al-Shabab's Attack at Westgate Mall: Somalia and Regional Instability."
36 "Statement by the Executive Secretary of IGAD Ambassador Mahboub M. Maalim on the successful neutralization of al-Shabab terrorist attack at the Westgate Mall and the regional way forward." See also: International Crisis Group, "Somalia: Countering Terrorism in a Failed State"; de Waal and Abed Salam, "Africa, Islamism and America's 'War on Terror.'"

Somalia's involvement in the international community and guides IGAD's involvement in Somalia."[37] In spite of these optimistic plans, the fact that IGAD continues to regularly address issues such as political instability in Somalia or the fate of the millions of Somali refugees and IDPs clearly indicates that these issues remained irresolvable to this day, and despite the presence of AMISOM and other East African forces, al-Shabaab presence and activities continue to extend in the areas beyond Mogadishu (and sometimes even there). A recent communiqué of IGAD expressed "grave concern that Al-Shabaab and other terrorist groups continue to pose a serious threat to the security, peace and stability of Somalia and the region."[38] According to Ingiriis:

> The question of negotiating a political settlement by sitting with Al Shabaab thus warrants serious considerations, because it is both crucial and critical. It is crucial because it may save the lives of many people who would otherwise be dead in the continuing insurgency activities of Al Shabaab. It is critical because it leads to a continuation of armed conflicts that have failed to resolve on the warfront… Without negotiating with Al-Shabaab, it is unlikely that the conflict will end but likely that Al Shabaab will continue controlling the remote rural areas outside of the center.[39]

The need for integrating as many factions as possible within the mediation process could be considered as one of the important lessons to be learned from IGAD's many decades of mediation process in Somalia. Yet, besides the issue of inclusiveness, another major issue, one that deals with separatism, also challenged IGAD's mediation efforts. Interestingly enough, the only two cases in Africa that challenged these notions, the separation of Eritrea from Ethiopia in 1993 and the separation of South Sudan from Sudan in 2011, occurred in the IGAD region. IGAD officials' rhetoric toward Somalia and Somaliland nonetheless continued to refer to the traditional post-colonial conventions of a "sovereign state" vs. "separatist area."

The final section of this chapter compares IGAD's attitudes toward Somaliland to its attitudes toward South Sudan, and specifically its attitudes toward the separatist aims in both countries. The importance of this comparison lies

37 Nairobi Forum, "IGAD and Somalia," 1.

38 IGAD, "Nairobi Declaration on Durable Solutions for Somali Refugees and Reintegration of Returnees in Somalia." See also: *Agence de Presse Africaine*, "Kenya to host special IGAD summit on Somali refugees," 24.

39 Ingiriis, "Building Peace from the Margins in Somalia: The Case for Political Settlement with Al-Shabaab," 16, 17.

in the fact that both Somaliland and South Sudan required recognition as independent political entities, yet only South Sudan was recognized by international, continental, and regional organizations, including IGAD. The roots of present-day Somaliland can be traced to the colonial partition of Somalia. Somaliland regards itself as the successor state to the former British Somaliland protectorate (which, in the form of what was the briefly independent State of Somaliland, united in July 1960 with the Trust Territory of Somaliland, the former Italian Somaliland, to form the Somali Republic). Moreover, Somaliland had a brief history as an internationally recognized independent state called Somaliland. This is one of the bases for Somaliland's claim for recognition as a separate state from Somalia.[40]

Thirty years passed between the independence of the Somali Republic and the declaration of the independence of Somaliland by Abdurahmaan Tuur, one of the Somali National Movement's (SNM) leaders. In the course of these extensively documented three decades,[41] the relations between the central government of Somalia and the region of Somaliland could only be described as turbulent, especially during the dictatorship phase of Siad Barre's regime, and much has been written about it.

The birth of present-day Somaliland coincided with the collapse of the Somali state. Kenneth Menkhaus attributes one of the reasons for the collapse to the fact that "Somalia" was never a single political entity, but actually comprised three political entities:

> Several regional and transregional authorities have come into existence in Somalia since 1990. Somaliland (a separatist state in the northwest) and Puntland (a non-secessionist, autonomous state in the arid northeast corner of the country) are the only two such entities that have achieved much functional capacity, but a number of others – the Rahanweyn Resistance Army's administration of Bay and Bakool regions in 1998–2002 and the Benadir Regional Authority in 1996 – showed some initial promise. Strictly speaking, most of these regional and transregional polities are or were essentially clan homelands, reflecting a Somali impulse to pursue a "Balkan solution" – or, more appropriate to the Somali context, "clanustans." Puntland's borders, for instance, are explicitly drawn along clan lines, encompassing the territory of the Harti clans in

40 Bereketeab, *Self-Determination and Secessionism in Somaliland and South Sudan: Challenges to Postcolonial State-Building*.

41 See, for example: Bradbury, *Becoming Somaliland: Reconstructing a Failed State*; Balthasar, "The Wars in the North and the Creation of Somaliland."

> the northeast and contested sections of Somaliland. Even authorities that appear to be based on a prewar regional unit are often thinly disguised clan polities.[42]

The conference held in Boroma in January 1993 soon after the self-proclaimed independence of Somaliland was considered a model of national dialogue: "It comprised 150 participants from all part of Somaliland, plus guests and observers, and was chaired by the eight members of the Guurti [the Council of Elders] in rotation."[43] Moreover, Somaliland was regarded by many as a model of new nation building in Africa, by virtue of its political stability, the lack of civil conflicts, and other factors. Kaplan referred to this model:

> Somaliland benefited from a comparatively homogeneous population, modest disparities in personal wealth, widespread fear of the south, and a lack of outside interference that might have undermined the accountability that was forced on its leaders. This cohesiveness – which sharply distinguishes Somaliland from Somalia and from most other African states – has combined with the enduring strength of traditional institutions of self-governance to mold a unique form of democracy. From the outset of Somaliland's independence movement, traditional democratic methods predominated in the efforts to create governing organs. The SNM was notable for its internal democratic practices, changing its leadership no fewer than five times in the nine years that it spent fighting the Siad Barre regime. A Council of Elders established during this time to resolve disputes and distribute food among the refugees quickly gained legitimacy, and the Council came to play a key role in promoting a process of representative decision making when the war ended. Within two years of the proclamation of independence, the ruling party SNM had turned power over to a civilian administration.[44]

To be sure, this idea of Somaliland as a model for African nation-state building was not accepted by many scholars, analysts, and observers, who argue against its militaristic nature, authoritarian government, uneven wealth sharing, and other undemocratic characteristics.[45] Yet, it is quite commonly agreed that

---

42 Menkhaus, "Governance without Government in Somalia: Spoilers, State Building, and the Politics of Coping," 83.

43 de Waal, *The Real Politics of the Horn of Africa: Money, War and the Business of Power*, 133.

44 Kaplan, "The Remarkable Story of Somaliland," 153.

45 For a detailed overview of the different views on Somaliland, see: Balthasar, "The Wars in the North and the Creation of Somaliland."

Somaliland functions much better than the neighboring Somalia in many areas including economic performance and political stability. One major example of Somaliland's superior performance concerns its successful attempts of disarmament. During 1994–1995, a national campaign of disarmament persuaded many citizens to cede their heavy and light weapons to the government representatives. According to de Waal, "The 1994–5 war did not therefore cause a general rush to arms, but rather a consolidation of arms and armed man under the government. Egal had more guns than money, and his war-fighting strategy was based on organized forces rather than patronage."[46] Also, in contrast to the inability of the South Sudanese government to effectively implement any form of centralized disarmament, and the far-reaching impact of weapons proliferation on the soaring internal violence, it is difficult to disregard the achievements of Somaliland's disarmament policy. One must wonder, then, why IGAD was so extensively and intensely involved in the mediation process between Sudan and South Sudan yet constantly ignored Somaliland's call for recognition and mediation with Somalia.

Ismail Wais, Special IGAD Envoy for South Sudan, compared the legitimacy of the South Sudan call for national recognition to the case of Somaliland. He claimed that, in contrast to Somaliland, the Sudanese government was able to execute a referendum on the independence of South Sudan.[47] When Mahboub Maalim, IGAD Executive Secretary was asked in 2013 how IGAD could be involved in conflict resolution between Somalia and Somaliland, he answered that, "Eventually, it will be the Somali people who will decide how they want to form their own government, and what type of government it will be."[48] This viewpoint was reaffirmed again at The 28th IGAD Extra Ordinary Summit, which was held on September 13, 2016 in Mogadishu, Somalia.[49] This viewpoint, to be sure, was rejected by Somaliland President Ahmed Mohamed Silanyo, who claimed:

> Despite our desire for peace in Somalia and readiness to help in any way as well as support for concerted international efforts, I take this opportunity to condemn some articles of the Communiqué by IGAD leaders in Mogadishu that pertains to the unity of Somalia. We perceive this article terming Somaliland as a self-ruling region of Somalia as not only a lie but

46 de Waal, *The Real Politics of the Horn of Africa: Money, War and the Business of Power*, 139.

47 Interview with Ambassador Ismail Wais, Special IGAD Envoy to South Sudan.

48 Maalim, "IGAD's Role in Stability and Diplomacy in the Horn of Africa," 8.

49 This was a historic event for Somalia as it has not hosted a high level summit in over 30 years. See: Communiqué of 28th IGAD Extraordinary Summit on Somalia.

> misconception of facts based misinformation thus far from facts and the reality on the ground. So, once again, let me reiterate and confirm to the world that Somaliland is a free, independent and sovereign country and not as misconstrued a region of Somalia under administration by the Somalia federal Government in Mogadishu.[50]

Yet, the factors that facilitated IGAD's recognition of South Sudan while hindering Somaliland in its pursuit of this objective are much more comprehensive than the issue of the people's consent through referendum. According to a confluence of historical, political, economic, and other factors, Somaliland seems to be a more "deserving" candidate for self-determination, compared to South Sudan. The fact that IGAD's attitudes toward Somaliland's self-proclaimed independence reflected "old-school" conventions concerning the sanctity of colonial borders and respect for the sovereignty of the African states[51] requires further research.[52] On a more practical level, it seems that the observations regarding the similarities and differences in the case of IGAD mediation efforts in Somalia, Sudan, South Sudan, and Somaliland will be applicable to future cases of separatism and claims for independence in the turbulent political atmosphere of IGAD region.

---

50 "President Ahmed Mohamed Silanyo Strongly Condemned a Communiqué Released by IGAD Leaders in Mogadishu."

51 See an elaborated discussion on this theme in Chapter 1; See also: Back, *Intervention and Sovereignty in Africa: Conflict Resolution and International Organisations in Darfur*, 7–25.

52 Bereketeab, *Self-Determination and Secessionism in Somaliland and South Sudan: Challenges to Postcolonial State-Building*, 16.

Conclusion

Referring to a quote from Victor Hugo, "Stronger than all armies is an idea whose time has come," Robert Lieberman claims that the challenge of "bringing ideas back into political science is one of the central issue facing the discipline."[1] He emphasizes challenges concerning institutional theories of politics, which suffer from common shortcomings such as "reductionism, the exogeneity of certain fundamental elements of political life, and a privileging of structure over agency."[2] This challenge, he claims, is especially relevant to the post-Cold War era, when changes such as the collapse of Communism and the spread of neoliberalism signaled a profound global ideological transformation. As this era was characterized by massive disorder and political change, it poses a significant challenge to theories of institutionalism, which tend to exhibit a bias toward finding and explaining stability in political arrangements, and minimizes the discussion on disorder. Leiberman suggests an alternative to a dichotomous view on order and chaos: The alternative to order and regularity is not necessarily chaos. "Rather, we can consider that any political moment or episode or outcome is situated within a *variety* of ordered institutional and ideological patterns, each with its own origins and history and each with its own logic and pace."[3]

As one of the main features of disorder in the post-Cold War Africa was the soaring number of conflicts, it is important to reconsider the role that regional organizations played in efforts resolve these conflicts, and analyze them in light of new theories of regionalism such as the New Regionalism Approach. According to Katete, this approach "argues that in the context of globalization the state has become unbundled, resulting in the strengthening of traditional non-state actors." As a result, the Weberian ideal does not apply to the state, and it is instead important to view other internal and external forces "as playing overlapping roles either in providing or undermine security, development and governance within a state."[4] This observation is important from a regional perspective, as the conventional dichotomy between intra-state and inter-state conflicts is no longer viable: "In a world so interdependent and closely linked together, such compartmentalization of conflicts is simplistic and unrealistic.

1 Lieberman, "Ideas, Institutions, and Political Order: Explaining Political Change," 679.
2 Ibid: 698.
3 Ibid: 701.
4 Katete, "The Regional Outcome of the Comprehensive Peace Agreement Five Years Down the Road: Are External Forces Playing a Progressive Role,?" 162, 3.

 | DOI:10.1163/9789004425323_009

Purely internal or international conflicts do not exist. Inter-state conflicts have internal causes, while so-called internal conflicts have international repercussions (like outflows of refugees and armed insurgencies into neighboring states) that cannot be ignored by the affected states."[5] One crucial aspect to consider in this context is the question of whether external actors such as regional countries can undermine conflict resolution efforts if they deem that the negotiated peace does not serve their national interests, as the follow case exemplifies.

The border dispute between Eritrea and Djibouti broke out in 2008 around an approximately 63-mile-long border between the two countries. Although this conflict could be considered marginal from a regional perspective, it still included many of the features commonly found in other interstate conflicts in the late twentieth and the two first decades of the twenty-first century, including a complicated legacy of colonial borders, proxy wars, and spillover threats.[6] Moreover, the success of third-party mediation (in this case, Qatari) to end the conflict in a relative short span of time serves as an interesting case study and offers a model of mediation in the region and beyond. In this context, Frank asks two questions that could be particularly relevant to mediation efforts discussed in this book: "First, what were the factors that led to the ripeness of the situation, allowing the Qataris to initiate mediation, and that were not present before? Second, does the regional organization as mediator present inherent difficulties not found in other types of third-party mediation, such as a single state, international organization, or nongovernmental organization?"[7]

Chapter 3 in this book discussed Zartman's concept of "ripeness for resolution." Zartman claimed that ripeness occurs when, in the life cycle of a conflict, the parties considered the mediation process as a better option for their interests than the continuation of the conflict.[8] Zartman subsequently added the notion that circumstances are ripe "when the parties find themselves locked in a conflict from which they cannot escalate to victory and this deadlock is painful for both of them (although not necessarily in equal degrees or for the same

5 Munya, "The Organization of African Unity and Its Role in Regional Conflict Resolution and Dispute Settlement: A Critical Evaluation," 591. Although the author discussed conflict resolution and regionalism mainly during the Organization of African Unity era, many of his observations are still applicable until today.

6 For a detailed description of the development of this dispute, see: Frank, "Ripeness and the 2008 Djibouti-Eritrea Border Dispute," 121–6. See also Kornprobst, "The Management of Border Disputes in African Regional Subsystems: Comparing West Africa and the Horn of Africa."

7 Frank, *ibid.*, 115.

8 Zartman, *Ripe for Resolution: Conflict and Intervention in Africa*, 263–4.

reasons), they seek a way out."[9] This theory was reconsidered by Pruitt, whose "readiness theory" focused on elements of optimism and the parties' motivation to end the conflict. He defined motivation as "the realization by that unilateral tactics are unworkable, and that allies are pressing for an end to the conflict and for negotiation," and claimed that these elements are important variables in a "compensatory model in which a decrease in one variable can be offset by an increase in the other. This provides for distinctions between parties and situations."[10] Was IGAD's mediation role in Sudan and South Sudan related to moments of ripeness or readiness, or was it the organization's cumulative experience as a mediator in intrastate and interstate regional conflicts, that created a series of successes and failures in that process?

Over a period of approximately four decades, IGAD mediation efforts coincided with many moments of ripeness and readiness in these conflicts, and other moments in which the belligerent parties withdrew from the mediation, sometimes even causing an escalation in the conflict in question. In 2000, Adar reviewed IGAD's achievements in the mediation process in Sudan, and predicted that "the transformation of IGAD into IGO responsible for conflict resolution, prevention and management has given the organization incentives on the Sudanese peace process. It is fair to argue that a consensus is emerging among the belligerent with respect to the option of self-determination for the South."[11] Five additional years were, however, required before the parties were ready to sign the CPA.

Indeed, in late 2004 and early 2005, IGAD was proving to be unusually adept at performing its new conflict-resolution role, not just in Sudan, but also in Somalia. Two IGAD settlements within three months appeared to be a remarkable accomplishment, especially when taking into consideration that both settlements addressed long, complex, and intractable conflicts that had defied previous attempts to secure a peaceful settlement. By 2009, Sally Healy claimed:

> Looked at in the context of the overall regional conflict environment, it is clear that IGAD is far from providing an institutional basis for regional security in the Horn of Africa. The region continues to experience exceptionally high levels of violent conflict. The relatively successful mediations in Sudan and Somalia in 2004 and 2005 stand alongside IGAD's inability to prevent or resolve the Ethiopia-Eritrea war of 1998–2000 or to deal with violent conflict in Darfur and rumbling conflicts in Northern

9 Zartman, "Ripeness: The Hurting Stalemate and Beyond," 228.
10 Quoted in Frank, "Ripeness and the 2008 Djibouti-Eritrea Border Dispute," 117.
11 Adar, "Conflict Resolution in a Turbulent Region," 61.

> Uganda and Eastern Ethiopia. Even during the Sudanese and Somali peace processes IGAD member states demonstrated their willingness to prepare for and engage in war at the same time as organising for peace.[12]

Healy also pointed to the authoritarian culture of the region's political leaders who manipulate IGAD activities to fit their own interests and needs, and, on the other hand, to the absence of a local powerful hegemon, such as South Africa and Nigeria in their respective regions, that could handle the mediation process with greater decisiveness. The significance of mediating in a regional conflict in regions with and without a hegemonic power was discussed in detail in Chapter 1. In the absence of a regional hegemon "to influence and guide the cooperation of the member states, a consensus of the member states is required for a regional cooperation to be effective."[13] Berhe claimed that although Ethiopia, Kenya, and Sudan have several elements of power, none them have the ability to act as a hegemonic regional power.

Khadiagala pointed to many similarities between mediation processes in regions with and without a hegemonic power. For example, he points to the similarities in the roles of General Sumbeiywo from Kenya and former President Zuma from South Africa in their respective mediation efforts:

> Moi appointed Sumbeiywo, a close confidant, who put his imprimatur on the IGAD Secretariat, transforming it into an institution that symbolized the convergence of invitational and organizational power. Similarity, after taking over from Mandela, former South African Deputy President Zuma quickly established his authority over Burundi's parties. Both Sumbeiywo and Zuma grew in their roles as mediators by making themselves useful and indispensable to the parties, and by skillful management of regional and international pressures, they succeeded in husbanding major agreements.[14]

Despite the optimism expressed by Khadiagala, the signing of the CPA in 2005 was by no means the end of the need for IGAD mediation efforts. The loopholes of the agreement and the reversals in its implementation, both during

12 Healy, "Peacemaking in the Midst of War: An Assessment of IGAD'S Contribution to Regional Security," 11–12.

13 Berhe, "Regional Peace and Security Cooperation under the Intergovernmental Authority on Development: Development and Challenges," 111.

14 Khadiagala, *Meddlers or Mediators? African Interveners in Civil Conflicts in Eastern Africa*, 256.

the interim period and after South Sudan independence, are described in detail in Chapter 3. One of the major shortcomings of the IGAD-brokered agreement was its lack of inclusivity, both of Sudan's "other regions" such as Darfur, the Blue Nile, South Kordofan, and Abyei, and of many elements of South Sudanese society, such as the numerous opposition groups to the SPLM/A.[15] IGAD took various steps to create the semblance of an inclusive negotiation process that involved as many ethnic, religious, generation, and gender groups as possible, for example by organizing a symposium on the fate of the elections that included elders, women, and youth. In practice, most of this forum's recommendations were effectively ignored.[16] In this context, Alex de Waal argued, "IGAD, designated as mediator, adopted a peacemaking formula based on reflex rather than reflection."[17] Wild, Jok, and Pate support and extend this argument, claiming that "Neither the 2005 Comprehensive Peace Agreement nor the 2015 Agreement on the Resolution of the Conflict in South Sudan included substantive provisions to address the grievances and crucial role of non-state actors and informal armed groups such as the Nuer White Army or the Dinka *titweng/gelweng* in the larger political conflict."[18] The exclusion of many groups in South Sudan from essential negotiations processes that determined their fate in the newborn nation, combined with the increasing fragmentation of South Sudanese society, were two of the many factors that were responsible for the eruption of a violent conflict shortly after its independence. According to Stringham and Forney:

> What is undeniable is that the ostensibly successful peace treaties of the past such as the CPA (or the Addis Ababa Agreement of 1972 that 'ended' Sudan's first civil war) 'worked' for a few years but have not created lasting peace. Disputes in Juba can certainly encourage violence but the profound wealth inequalities between the rural majority and certain urban centers (Bor in 1991, Nasir in 1993, and in Malakal, Bor and Bentiu in 2013). are also an important part of the history of South Sudan's civil wars and a central reason why parochial civilian militias have continued to conclude that it pays to rebel.[19]

15 Interview with Mearuf Nurhusein.
16 Interview with an IGAD official.
17 de Waal, "The Price of South Sudan's Independence," 196.
18 Wild, Jok, and Pate, "The Militarization of Cattle Raiding in South Sudan: How a Traditional Practice Became a Tool for Political Violence,"8.
19 Stringham and Forney, "It Takes a Village to Raise a Militia: Local Politics, the Nuer White Army, and South Sudan's Civil Wars," 197.

The complexity of IGAD's mediation efforts in South Sudan, and specifically since the outbreak of the civil war in December 2013, was discussed in detail in Chapters 4 and 5. Following this discussion, two questions are warranted. First, in the case of South Sudan, was the concept of "African 'sub-regional' solutions to African 'sub-regional' problems"[20] more effective (or at least more feasible) compared with the alternatives? Second, what were the relations between conflict resolution and the demand for democracy, and how did IGAD respond to recent developments in the context in the continent and in the region, with reference to its own mediation efforts in South Sudan?

As for the first question, it seems that the regional organization's proximity to the locus of the conflict area had several advantages in terms of a more accurate understanding of the situation and the composition of the rival factions, and facilitated immediate response to the events. Presumably, IGAD would be better equipped to map South Sudan's rivaling factions than other mediators from outside the region. A better understanding of their interests, alliances, and rivalries would enhance the organization's ability to facilitate a dialogue between them.[21]

However, the proximity between the regional organization and the locus of the conflict can be considered a double-edged sword, as both also inject foreign interests into the local conflict, and encourage the rivaling parties to use foreign resources for their own interests. According to Coggins, in secessionist conflicts, separatist groups actively enlist the support of strong international and regional powers while harnessing the support of external powers sympathetic to their cause. This power relation is not addressed in mediation analysis. She claims that in secessionist literature, it is recognized that "Sensing the potential for political recognition, for example, may encourage secessionist movements to continue fighting rather than accept seemingly generous settlements from their home states."[22]

This was the case concerning the interests of IGAD states in the mediation process between the North and the South, and subsequently between the rival parties in South Sudan, discussed in detail in various chapters of this book. Although several IGAD members supported Salva Kiir's claims to continuing dominance in the state, and others supported Riek Machar's claims against it,

20 Originally mentioned by Adar, "Conflict Resolution in a Turbulent Region: The Case of the Intergovernmental Authority on Development (IGAD) in Sudan," 43.

21 Interview with Dr. Sunday Okello.

22 Coggins, "Friends in High Places: International Politics and the Emergence of States from Secessionism," 433–467.

IGAD was generally considered pro-Kiir.[23] Machar's supporters even recently accused IGAD of colluding on Machar's deportation to South Africa, claiming,

> It is hereby submitted that the judgment in that political kangaroo court of IGAD is fraught with gross violation of international humanitarian and human right law, violation of CoHA, double standards and conflict of interest legally and morally disqualifying the regional organization from its current status as a mediator in the peace process to resolve the ongoing conflict in South Sudan. In the light of this overwhelming credibility crisis, the IGAD must expressly take the following actions to save whatever little credibility it might still have to continue with mediating the peace process in South Sudan.[24]

Cliffe commented that "Granted that several countries share these problems, what can be added to their solution by tackling them at the regional as opposed to the national or community level? Or to put in slightly different terms: common problems do not necessarily or inevitably lead to regional partnership."[25] Ylönen claimed that IGAD's role and successes in mediating in local conflicts can be attributed to the support of foreign interests that, for various reasons, wished to promote the idea of "African solutions to African problems," and the resulting notion of IGAD "as a successful example of African regionalism."[26] On a more optimistic note, Khadiagala claimed that "Proponents of strong regionalism also allege that with more African ownership of its governance and security problems, the continent should be able to elicit more resources and greater commitments from international partners for mutually beneficial initiatives."[27]

Indeed, IGAD's interventions in Sudan, South Sudan, and Somalia, which were compared in Chapter 6, stressed the fact that IGAD relied, and continues to rely, substantially on the support of the broader international system, notably the AU, the UN, and the international donor community, yet issues such as defining the responsibilities of these organizations and their methods of collaboration, warrant further research. Bereketeab claims that the AU and the UN erred when they left the mediation task to IGAD exclusively: "Trusting corrupt, tribal and ineffective governments to implement a peace deal is a big

23 Interview with Kenyan Diplomat.
24 Kuol, "South Sudan Crisis: Machar vs. IGAD."
25 Cliffe, "Regional dimensions of conflict in the Horn of Africa," 104.
26 Ylönen, "Security regionalism and flaws of externally forged peace in Sudan," 35.
27 Khadiagala, "Regional Cooperation on Democratization and Conflict Management in Africa," 4.

mistake. A clear and steadfast mediation, unswerving stand, principled, targeted and serious sanctions would put an end to the suffering of the people of South Sudan."[28] Ylönen also mentions IGAD's organizational inability to tackle emergency humanitarian situations, and especially food crises.[29] This observation of the relation between IGAD's mediation efforts and further escalation of the humanitarian situation on the ground in general, and the recurrent pattern of ceasefire agreements that were signed and not implemented, remains applicable today, as recently reported by an IRIN correspondent:

> The civil war, now in its fifth year, has claimed tens of thousands of lives, displaced more than four million people – either to other parts of South Sudan or to neighboring countries – and, along with poor governance, done untold damage to the oil-rich country's economy. On 27 June, President Salva Kiir and his rival Riek Machar agreed that a "permanent" ceasefire would come into effect within 72 hours, and that humanitarian corridors would be opened up. But, like numerous previous ceasefires, it was violated almost before the ink dried. The latest agreement builds on a flawed 2015 peace accord that has done nothing to end the conflict, and many analysts believe it is also destined to fail. Without lasting peace, international aid organisations fear little progress can be made to help stem hunger in the world's newest country, which has one of the world's worst levels of food security (access to enough nutritious food for a healthy life).[30]

Notwithstanding the justified criticism against IGAD's role as mediator (and this relates to the second question), it is important to enlarge our scope and view the issue from the broader perspective of an emerging African peace and security architecture. Broadly speaking, this new approach was consolidated with the establishment of the AU and the PSC. Its guiding principles are based on commitment to long-standing principles such as respect for territorial integrity, sanctity of boundaries, and non-interference; but also include more concrete definitions for prevention and reduction of intra-state conflicts,

28 Bereketeab, "The Collapse of IGAD Peace Mediation in the Current South Sudan Civil War: When National Interest Dictates Peace Mediation," 161.

29 Ylönen, "Security regionalism and flaws of externally forged peace in Sudan," 35.

30 IRIN, Stephanie Glinski. "'The Conflict Must End': Fighting Threatens to Drive Up Hunger in South Sudan's Lean Season."

including "increase in human rights violations in a polity"[31] and strengthening of the cooperation between continental and regional organizations on issues that require an interventionist approach. This approach became increasingly widespread in the first two decades of the twentieth century.[32] Alongside the emerging peace and security architecture, the AU also promoted an agenda of shared values under the title of African Governance Architecture (AGA), which "seeks to foster operational linkages by harmonizing existing governance institutions and mechanisms. The AGA is also engaged in advocacy campaigns to ensure that member states implement the normative frameworks and imbed the values of constitutionalism in national governance practices."[33]

This was the case with respect to the combined operations of ECOWAS and the AU in Cotê d'Ivoire in 2011. Following incumbent president Laurent Gbagbo's refusal to recognize the victory of the Northern contender Alassane Ouattara in the country's November 2010 elections, the PSC suspended the Cotê d'Ivoire from all AU activities, and declared its unequivocal support for the Ivorian people's right to determine their own political future. The organization nonetheless tended toward a conciliatory approach. ECOWAS, on its part, proved to be much more unflagging in its support for democratic change based on the choice of the Ivorian people: It rejected any compromise between the parties and threatened the use of force if President Gbagbo refused to accept the results announced by the Ivorian electoral commission chief. Ultimately, cooperation between ECOWAS[34] and the AU led to nomination of the elected president and has so far prevented recurrence of the civil war in Cotê d'Ivoire.

Cases of regional intervention in power transitions within states have become increasingly frequent in recent years. The stepping down of long-serving autocrats such as President Yahya Jammeh of Gambia in early 2017 would probably not have occurred without the active intervention of ECOWAS, and the same is true for the case of SADC's intervention in the withdrawal of the longtime ruler of Zimbabwe, President Robert Mugabe, from power later that year (although this intervention is considered to be more controversial).[35]

31 African Union, Report on the Status of the Establishment of the Continental Peace and Security Architecture. See also: Engel and Gomes Porto, *Africa's New Peace and Security Architecture, Promoting Norms, Institutionalizing Solutions*, 212–17.

32 Back, "The Emerging Role of African Regional Organizations in Enforcing Electoral Results."

33 Khadiagala, "Regional Cooperation on Democratization and Conflict Management in Africa," 7.

34 Yabi, "Keeping the Peace in Electoral Conflicts: The Role of ECOWAS, UNOCI and the International Community in Côte d'Ivoire."

35 *Quartz Africa,* "These Nine Charts Tell You What's in Store for Africa in 2018."

The discourse on power transitions, elections, and democratization, which is "alive and kicking" throughout Africa,[36] is particularly relevant to the case of South Sudan, the continent's newest nation. As mentioned in Chapter 4, tensions regarding democratization and transitions of power were among the reasons for the eruption of the conflict in December 2013. Several months later, upon his return from Addis Ababa where he signed a framework agreement on a ceasefire, South Sudan's President Salva Kiir declared immediately upon his landing in Juba airport that "Elections will be not held in 2015 because reconciliation between the people will have to take time." In an interview to the state-run South Sudan Television he added, "The processes will need no less than two years, so we decided that the next general elections [will] be held in 2017 so that there is [enough] time for preparations."[37] It should be noted that by the time of the writing of this chapter, the general elections scheduled for July 2018 had been postponed yet again.[38]

The case of IGAD's failure to make a clear statement on South Sudan's lack of commitment to democracy and power transition seem rather surprising if we take a historical perspective, and remember the organization's commitment to the right to conduct elections in Sudan in 2010, which were the precondition for South Sudan's referendum and independence. Yet, in terms of the interrelations between conflict resolution and democracy, it should be recalled that IGAD faced a particularly turbulent region. East Africa, and particularly the Horn of Africa, has a poor record of democratization, as well as a history of mutual destabilization and distrust. According to Dersso:

> This poor record coupled with the scant attention given to governance and human rights in the IGAD Agreement have undermined cooperation for promoting good governance and nurturing democracy within the framework of IGAD. Accordingly, as a result of this, IGAD made very little progress in undertaking activities in the areas of democratic governance, human rights, and rule of law. The body is indeed lagging behind other regional groupings, most notably the Southern African Development Community (SADC) and the Economic Community of West African States (ECOWAS), in terms of developing effective normative and institutional infrastructure in this area. Accordingly, unlike these other regions, no mechanism or practice has emerged in the region to sanction

36 See, for example: Brookings Africa, Mbaku, "Elections in Africa in 2018: Lessons from Kenya's 2017 Electoral Experiences."

37 *Sudan Tribune*, "South Sudan President Delays 2015 General Elections."

38 *Sudan Tribune*, "IGAD Suspends South Sudan Revitalization Talks."

or even investigate major democratic and human rights deficits in member countries.[39]

This book focuses mainly on IGAD's mediation efforts in Sudan and South Sudan (and briefly addressed its role as mediator in the conflict in Somalia). Notably, another regional organization exists: The East Africa Community (EAC) is an intergovernmental organization comprising six member states in the African Great Lakes region in eastern Africa: Burundi, Kenya, Rwanda, Tanzania, Uganda, and South Sudan (which joined the organization in 2016). Compared to IGAD, which focused on conflict resolution and environmental issues, such as migration priorities, EAC's attention is more strongly directed to economic interests. As such, the two regional organizations have different opinions on issues such as imposition of sanctions on the South Sudan government.[40] At the same time, they share many common interests that inform their policies on addressing the underlying causes of the grave conflicts in the region, such as monitoring of small arms and light weapons, borders, pastoralists, and cattle raiding.[41] Although these issues were always part and parcel of the dynamic between the region's communities, today, however, "the ready availability of arms and the incorporation of this practice into a larger political conflict in South Sudan have intensified the violence to unprecedentedly deadly levels. Raiders who once mounted attacks with spears are now armed with AK-47s available for as little as the price of two cows."[42] As argued earlier, a better acquaintance of regional players using traditional forms of mediation and reconciliation might create better options for conflict resolution in the region.[43] Further research might analyze and compare information sharing and shared policymaking between these two organizations, and potentially offer insights on optimizing cooperation between them.

Dramatic events often change the geopolitical landscape of the IGAD region. One recent example is the peace agreement signed by Ethiopia and

---

39 Dersso, "East Africa and the Intergovernmental Authority on Development: Mapping Multilateralism in Transition," 11.

40 Obonyo, "Peace in South Sudan Critical to Regional Stability."

41 In effect, in May 2001 the organizations signed a draft joint protocol on these issues. See: Juma, "The Intergovernmental Authority on Development and the East African Community," 243.

42 Wild, Jok, and Pate, "The Militarization of Cattle Raiding in South Sudan: How a Traditional Practice Became a Tool for Political Violence," 1–2.

43 According to Wild et al. (*ibid.*, 7), use of traditional mediation form of *dia*(blodwealt payments common in Sudan) could serve as bridge to reconciliation between the Dinka and the Nuer in South Sudan.

IGAD

AUTORITÉ INTERGOUVERNEMENTALE
POUR LE DÉVELOPPEMENT

REVITALISED AGREEMENT ON THE RESOLUTION OF THE CONFLICT IN THE REPUBLIC OF SOUTH SUDAN (R-ARCSS)

ADDIS ABABA, ETHIOPIA

12 SEPTEMBER 2018

FIGURE 1 Signed Revitalized Agreement on the Resolution of the Conflict in South Sudan, 2018
Link to the entire agreement: https://igad.int/programs/115-south-sudan-office/1950-signed-revitalized-agreement-on-the-resolution-of-the-conflict-in-south-sudan

Eritrea,[44] two rival states that have been battling for over two decades. IGAD's institutional experience accumulated over many years of active mediation in East Africa, marked by both successes and failures, will most likely continue to be required in this region, where African states are painfully aware of the regional and continental consequences of new conflicts that continue to erupt with no end in sight.

44 *Africa News*, "Ethiopia-Eritrea Peace Deal Boost for Regional Security."

Epilogue

Since the signing on the Revitalized Agreement on the Resolution of the Conflict in the Republic of South Sudan (R-ARCSS), IGAD efforts to implement the agreement continue. These continuing efforts reveal that although some of the old shortcomings of IGAD mediation patterns persist, some achievements and breakthroughs in the process are evident. The agreement stipulates that its implementation will be performed in two stages: an eight-month pre-transitional phase and a three-year implementation phase: the three-year period of a Revitalised Transnational Government of National Unity will then to be followed by national elections.[1] The main issues that should be clarified during the transition to implementation include "the resolution of the number of states and their boundaries; the review and drafting of key legislation, the incorporation of the Revitalized Agreement into the Transitional Constitution; and the cantonment, training and redeployment of unified forces."[2] In light of these recent developments in IGAD's mediation efforts between the rival parties in South Sudan, how should be it be assessed?

From a critical point of view, it is reasonable to claim that IGAD's mediation efforts were not sufficiently firm as to compel South Sudan's ruling elites to assume a genuine commitment to transition of power and democratization. Indeed, it is disconcerting to see that not only were no national elections held eight years after the country's independence, but the recent agreement between the rival parties, brokered by IGAD, allows the parties several more years without a genuine transition of power (as noted above). Arguably, IGAD reflects its member states' ambivalence toward the transition of power and democratization processes in their own homelands.

The best recent example of such ambivalence is related to the dramatic events that occurred in Sudan when the widespread protest movement led to the overthrow of the longstanding President Omar al-Bashir on 19 April 2019. Although IGAD's mediators, including Ethiopian Prime Minister Abyi Ahmed in particular, were actively involved in the mediations between the rival factions in Sudan,[3] the transition of power in Sudan remains unresolved. Since Sudan under al-Bashir was a major force in IGAD's mediation efforts in South

1 Tombe, "Revitalising the Peace in South Sudan: Assessing the State of the Pre-Transitional Phase," 1

2 UN Security Council, "Situation in South Sudan: Report of the Secretary-General," 14 June 2019.

3 UN Security Council, "UN Chief Welcomes Power-Sharing Deal between Sudanese Military and Opposition," 5 July 2019.

 | DOI:10.1163/9789004425323_010

Sudan, time will tell what position the new regime in Sudan will adopt on this issue:

> Moreover, as was claimed repeatedly throughout this book, regional interests in South Sudan were determining factors in the regional states' attitudes toward the mediation process. This is the main claim of Mahmood Mamdani, who criticized the regional states' involvement in South Sudan for leading to the total fragmentation of the newborn state: South Sudan is on its way to becoming an informal protectorate of Sudan and Uganda. By formally acknowledging them as "guarantors," the agreement recognizes their strategic role in determining the future of South Sudan Ugandan troops are physically present to support Mr. Kiir's faction, and Sudan provides critical support to opposition groups, including those led by Mr. Machar. South Sudan will likely turn into a tribally fragmented society. The state will reflect this fragmentation and will in turn deepen the societal fragmentation.[4]

From a more positive perspective it is possible to identity several successful aspects of IGAD's continued mediation efforts in South Sudan, such as the various steps it takes to create a semblance of an inclusive negotiation process that involves as many ethnic, religious, generation, and gender groups as possible, as mentioned in a recent UNMISS report:

> The IGAD Special Envoy for South Sudan, Ismail Wais also continued his outreach to key individuals and groups outside the peace process. The Special Envoy met with the leader of the South Sudan United Front/Army, General Paul Malong, from 11 to 13 March. Given General Malong's willingness to join the peace process, efforts are under way to facilitate negotiations with the incumbent Government. The Special Envoy also met with the leader of the National Salvation Front and the umbrella group South Sudan National Democratic Alliance, Thomas Cirillo, on 8 and 14 March.[5]

Although these talks have yielded little so far, and the gaps separation the demands of the various factions remain substantial, the efforts to create a more inclusive process of mediation are important in itself. As argued earlier, in

4 Mahmood Mamdani, "The Trouble with South Sudan's New Peace Deal," Sept. 24, 2018.

5 UN Security Council, "Situation in South Sudan: Report of the Secretary-General, 14 June 2019": 2.

many cases the inclusion of political or civil factions that tend to feel marginalized by the mediation process tend to be a very important component in determining its success or failure.

Furthermore, many indicators point to the fact that the situation in South Sudan is stabilizing. A recent UNMISS report on the situation in South Sudan noted the decreasing levels of violence in many areas, as well as preliminary indications of an economic e recovery.[6] The report mentions IGAD's contribution to this process of stabilization, referring in particular to its fruitful cooperation with other forces involved in peace building efforts, such as UNMISS itself and the African Union.[7] Although these early signs of stabilization and recovery still required a very cautious outlook, they nonetheless might be interpreted an encouraging indications of the evolving power of regional mediation in ongoing and devastating conflicts.

6 Ibid: 4–5.
7 Ibid: 14.

Bibliography

Abbink, Jon. "Dervishes, 'moryaan' and Freedom Fighters: Cycles of Rebellion and the Fragmentation of Somali Society, 1900–2000". In *Rethinking Resistance: Revolt and violence in African history*, edited by Jon Abbink, Mirjamde Bruijn, and Klaas van Walraven, 328–56. Leiden: Brill, 2003.

Aboagye, Festus B. and Alhaji M.S. Bah, editors. *Tortuous Road to Peace: The Dynamics of Regional, UN and International Interventions in Liberia.* Pretoria: Institute for Security Studies, 2005.

Abraham, Kinfe. *Somalia Calling: The Crisis of Statehood and the Quest for Peace.* Addis Ababa: EIIPD, 2002.

"Abyei Referendum Enters Second Day." *al-Jazeera News*, October 28, 2013. https://www.aljazeera.com/news/africa/2013/10/sudan-abyei-referendum-enters-second-day-201310289549134671.html.

Adar, Korwa G. "Conflict Resolution in a Turbulent Region: The Case of the Intergovernmental Authority on Development (IGAD) in Sudan." *African Journal of Conflict Resolution*, 1, no. 2 (2000): 39–65.

Adebajo, Adekeye. *Building Peace in West Africa: Liberia, Sierra Leone, and Guinea-Bissau.* Boulder, CO: Lynne Rienner Publishers, 2002.

Adedajo, Adekeye. "The Peacekeeping Travails of the AU and the Regional Economic Communities." In *The African Union and its Institutions*, edited by John Akokpari, Angela Ndinga-Muvumba, and Tim Murith, 131–62. Auckland Park, South Africa: Fanele, 2008.

Adedajo, Adekeye and Christopher Landsberg. "The Heirs of Nkrumah: Africa's New Interventionists." *Pugwash Occasional Papers* 2, no. 1 (2000): 65–90.

Adedajo, Adekeye and Christopher Landsberg, "South Africa and Nigeria as Regional Hegemons." In *From Cape to Congo: Southern Africa's Evolving Security Challenges*, edited by Mwesiga Baregu and Christopher Landsberg, 171–204. Boulder, CO: Lynne Reiner Publishers, 2003.

Adekele, Ademola. "The Politics and Diplomacy of Peacekeeping in West Africa: The ECOWAS Operation in Liberia." *Journal of Modern African Studies* 33, no. 4 (1995): 569–93.

Adibe, Clement E. "The Liberian Conflict and the ECOWAS-UN Partnership." *Third World Quarterly* 18, no. 3 (1997): 471–88.

Africa News. "Sudan; AU Commission Chairman Urges Country to Rise to Referendum Challenge in 2011." September 27, 2010.

Africa News. "Ethiopia-Eritrea Peace Deal Boost for Regional Security." July 10, 2018. http://www.africanews.com/2018/07/10/ethiopia-eritrea-peace-deal-boost-for-regional-peace-au-eu/.

Africa Research Bulletin. "IGAD Decision on South Sudan Force." March 1–31, 2014.

Agence de Presse Africaine (APA *news*). "Kenya to Host Special IGAD Summit on Somali Refugees." March 24, 2017.

Amnesty International. "Looking for Justice: Recommendations for the Establishment of the Hybrid Court for South Sudan." October 2016. https://www.amnesty.org/download/Documents/AFR6547422016ENGLISH.PDF.

Andemariam, Senai. "In, Out or at the Gate? The Predicament on Eritrea's Membership and Participation Status in IGAD." *Journal of African Law* 59, no. 2 (2015): 355–79.

Aning, Emmanuel K. "The Challenge of Civil Wars to Multilateral Interventions – UN, ECOWAS, and Complex Political Emergencies in West Africa: A Critical Analysis." *Asian and African Studies* 4, nos. 1–2 (2005): 1–20.

Annan, Kofi A. "Two concepts of Sovereignty". *The Economist* 18, no. 9(1999). https://www.economist.com/international/1999/09/16/two-concepts-of-sovereignty.

[*The*] *Anya-Nya Struggle: Background and Objectives*. London: South Sudan Resistance Movement, 1971. http://southsudanhumanitarianproject.com/wp-content/uploads/sites/21/formidable/South-Sudan-Resistance-Movement-Unknown-The-Anya-Nya-Struggle-Background-And-Objectives.pdf2-annotated.pdf.

Apuuli Phillip, Kasaija. "IGAD's Mediation in the Current South Sudan Conflict: Prospects and Challenges." *African Security* 8, no. 2 (2015): 120–45.

Awolich Abraham A. "The Unwarranted Carnage in South Sudan." *The Sudd Institute Policy Brief*, February 13, 2014: 1.

Bach, Daniel C. "The Politics of West African Economic Co-Operation: C.E.A.O. and E.C.O.W.A.S." *The Journal of Modern African Studies* 21, no. 4 (1983): 605–23.

Back, Irit. "Al-Shabab's Attack at Westgate Mall: Somalia and Regional Instability." *Tel Aviv Notes* 7, no. 19 (2013): 1–4. https://dayan.org/content/tel-aviv-notes-al-shababs-attack-westgate-mall-somalia-and-regional-instability

Back, Irit. "IGAD, Sudan and South Sudan: Achievements and Setbacks of Regional Mediation." *Journal of the Middle East and Africa* 7, no. 2 (2016): 141–55.

Back, Irit. *Intervention and Sovereignty in Africa: Conflict Resolution and International Organisations in Darfur*. London: I.B. Tauris, 2015.

Back, Irit, "South Sudan, Six Months On." *Tel Aviv Notes* 6, no. 1 (2012): 1.

Back, Irit. "The Emerging Role of African Regional Organizations in Enforcing Electoral Results." *Ifriqiya* 2, no. 9, January 23, 2017.

Balthasar, Dominic. "The Wars in the North and the Creation of Somaliland." *Reinventing Peace* October 28, 2013. https://sites.tufts.edu/reinventingpeace/2013/10/28/the-wars-in-the-north-and-the-creation-of-somaliland/

Baregu, Mwesiga. "Economic and Military Security." In *From Cape to Congo: Southern Africa's Evolving Security Challenges*, edited by Mwesiga Baregu and Christopher Landsberg, 19–30. Boulder, CO: Lynne Reiner Publishers, 2003.

Baregu, Mwesiga and Christopher Landsburg. "Introduction." In *From Cape to Congo: Southern Africa's Evolving Security Challenges*, 1–18. Boulder, CO: Lynne Reiner Publishers, 2003.

Bariyo, Nicholas, "South Sudan's Debt Rises as Oil Ebbs: Oil Companies No Longer Want to Extend Advance Payments." *Wall Street Journal*, August 5, 2014. https://www.wsj.com/articles/south-sudans-debt-rises-as-oil-ebbs-1407280169.

Barltrop, Richard. *Darfur and the International Community: The Challenges of Conflict Resolution in Sudan*. London: I.B. Tauris, 2011.

Bentley, Kristina A. and Roger Southall. *An African Peace Process: Mandela, South Africa and Burundi*. Cape Town: HSRC Press, 2005.

Bereketeab, Redie. *Self-Determination and Secessionism in Somaliland and South Sudan: Challenges to Postcolonial State-Building*. Uppsala: Nordiska Afrikainstitutet, 2002.

Bereketeab, Redie. "The Collapse of IGAD Peace Mediation in the Current South Sudan Civil War: When National Interest Dictates Peace Mediation." *Journal of African Foreign Affairs* 4, no. 1–2 (2017): 147–64.

Bereketeab, Redie. "Why South Sudan Conflict is Proving Intractable." *Policy Note* 4, 2015. https://www.diva-portal.org/smash/get/diva2:796592/FULLTEXT01.pdf

Berhe, Mulugeta G. "Regional Peace and Security Cooperation under the Intergovernmental Authority on Development: Development and Challenges." *Eastern Africa Social Science Research Review* 30, no. 1 (2014): 105–31.

Botha, Anneli. "Who's Who in the Somali Quagmire?" *The African Org.* 2010, 9: 15–7.

Boutros-Ghali, Boutros. "An Agenda for Peace" (New York: United Nations, 1992). In *Supplement to an Agenda to Peace*, S/1995/1, January 3, 1995.

Bradbury, Mark. *Becoming Somaliland: Reconstructing a Failed State*. Bloomington: Indiana University Press, 2008.

Brons, Maria H. *Society, Security, Sovereignty and the State in Somalia: From Statelessness to Statelessness?* Utrecht: International Books, 2001.

Brookings Africa, Mbaku, John M. "Elections in Africa in 2018: Lessons from Kenya's 2017 electoral experiences." February 1, 2018. https://www.brookings.edu/blog/africa-in-focus/2018/02/01/foresight-africa-viewpoint-elections-in-africa-in-2018-lessons-from-kenyas-2017-electoral-experiences/?utm_campaign=Brookings%20Brief&utm_source=hs_email&utm_medium=email&utm_content=60397568

Brown, Leann. "Why Regional Economic Organizations Take on Conventional Security Tasks?" *ASPJ Africa and Francophonie* 6, no. 4 (2015): 5–20.

Cardoso, Nilton C.F. "Regional Security in the Horn of Africa: Conflicts, Agendas and Threats." *Brazilian Journal of African Studies* 1, no. 2 (2016): 131–65.

Carter Center. "Carter Center Urges Political Parties and Blue Nile Popular Consultation Commission to Ensure Genuine Dialogue on Key Issues in Blue Nile State." March 21, 2011. https://www.cartercenter.org/news/pr/sudan-032111.html

CCR. "The Peacebuilding role of Civil Society in South Sudan." *African Report* 243, December 20, 2016. file:///C:/Users/a/Desktop/vol55_peacebuilding_role_civil_society_southsudan_nov2016.pdf

Christensen, Katja H. "Conflict Early Warning and Response Mechanism in the Horn of Africa: IGAD as a Pioneer in Regional Conflict Prevention in Africa." October 2009. http://www.pcr.uu.se/digitalAssets/67/c_67531-l_1-k_conflict_early_warning__igad_as_pioneer_in_regional_conflict_prevention_in_africa__katja_h._christensen__mfs__2009.pdf

Cliffe, Lionel. "Regional Dimensions of Conflict in the Horn of Africa." *Third World Quarterly* 20, no. 1 (1999): 89–111.

Cohen, Roberta and Francis M. Deng. *Masses in Flights: The Global Crisis of Internal Displacement.* Washington, DC: Brookings Institution Press, 1998.

Collins, Robert O. *Civil Wars and Revolution in the Sudan: Essays on the Sudan, Southern Sudan, and Darfur, 1962–2004.* Preface by Francis Deng. Hollywood, CA: Tsehai Publishers, 2005.

Coltan, Congo and conflict: Polinares Case Study. The Hague Centre for Strategic Studies (HCSS) Report, 2013.

Craig, Jill. "Analysts: Absence of South Sudan President from IGAD Summit Problematic." *VOA News*, June 13 2017. https://www.voanews.com/a/analysts-say-absence-south-sudan-president-igad-summit-problematic/3898753.html

Crisis Group Africa. "Instruments of Pain (II): Conflict and Famine." *South Sudan Briefing* 124, April 26, 2017. https://d2071andvipowj.cloudfront.net/b124-instruments-of-pain-ii.pdf

Daily Nation (Nairobi). "Court Lifts President al-Bashir Arrest Warrant," February 17, 2018. https://www.nation.co.ke/news/africa/Court-lifts-President-al-Bashir-arrest-warrant/1066-4309472-k9n7xpz/index.html

Daly, M.W. "The Sudans in the Twenty-First Century." *African Studies Review* 55, no. 1 (2012): 205–10 (Review).

Danforth, John C. *Report to the President of the United States on the Outlook for Peace in Sudan*, April 26, 2002. http://pdf.usaid.gov/pdf_docs/Pcaab158.pdf

de Waal, Alex. "The Price of South Sudan's Independence." *Current History* 114 (2015): 194–96.

de Waal, Alex. *The Real Politics of the Horn of Africa: Money, War and the Business of Power.* Cambridge: Polity Press, 2015.

de Waal, Alex. "When Kleptocracy Becomes Insolvent: Brute Causes of the Civil War in South Sudan." *African Affairs* 113, no. 452 (2014): 347–69.

de Waal, Alex and A.H. Abed Salam. "Africa, Islamism and America's 'War on Terror'." In *Islamism and its Enemies in the Horn of Africa*, edited by Alex De Waal, 231–57. London: Hurst & Company, 2004.

Deng, Francis M. "Mediating the Sudanese Conflict: A Challenge for the IGADD." *CSIS Africa Notes* 169 (1995): 1–7.

Dersso, Solomon. "East Africa and the Intergovernmental Authority on Development: Mapping Multilateralism in Transition." New York: International Peace Institute,

October 2014. https://www.ipinst.org/wp-content/uploads/publications/ipi_e_pub_igad.pdf

Dessu, Meressa K. "IGAD's initiative is encouraging, but it's unlikely to overcome obstacles that have bedeviled previous efforts." Tel-Aviv: Institute for Security Studies, December 8, 2017. https://issafrica.org/iss-today/can-south-sudans-peace-agreement-be-revitalised

Duffield, Mark. *Global Governance and the New Wars: The Merging of Development and Security*. London and New York: Zed Books, 2001.

Dumo, Denis. "South Sudan Sentences Rebel Leader's Spokesman to Death." *Reuters*, February 12, 2018. https://www.reuters.com/article/us-southsudan-trial/south-sudan-sentences-rebel-leaders-spokesman-to-death-idUSKBN1FW1LO

El-Effendi, Abedl Wahab. "The Impasse in the IGAD Peace Process for Sudan: The Limits of Regional Peacemaking." *African Affairs* 100 (2001): 581–99.

Elamu, Denis. "News Analysis: South Sudan May Miss 2018 Elections." *Xinhua* February 20, 2017. http://www.xinhuanet.com/english/2017-02/20/c_136071359.htm

Engel, Ulf and João Gomes Porto, editors. *Africa's New Peace and Security Architecture: Promoting Norms, Institutionalizing Solutions*. Aldershot: Ashgate, 2011.

Erlich, Haggai. *Islam and Christianity in the Horn of Africa: Somalia, Ethiopia and Sudan*. Boulder, CO: Lynne Rienner Publishers, 2010.

Federal Democratic Republic of Ethiopia. "A Week in the Horn." October 6, 2017. http://www.ethiopianembassy.net/wp-content/uploads/2017/10/A-Week-in-the-Horn-06.10.2017.pdf

Francis, David J. *Uniting Africa: Building Regional Peace and Security Systems*. London: Ashgate, 2006.

Frank, Kevin K. "Ripeness and the 2008 Djibouti-Eritrea Border Dispute." *Northeast African Studies* 15, no. 1 (2015): 113–38.

Garang, John. *John Garang Speaks*. London: KPI, 1987.

Garang, John and Mansūr Khālid. *The Call for Democracy in Sudan*. London: Kegan Paul International, 1987.

Gberie, A. Lansana. *A Dirty War in West Africa: The RUF and the Destruction of Sierra Leone*. Bloomington and Indianapolis: Indiana University Press, 2005.

Genser, Jared. "The United Nations Security Council's Implementation of the Responsibility to Protect: A Review of Past Interventions and Recommendations for Improvement." *Chicago Journal of International Law* 18, no. 2 (2018): 420–501.

Gettelman, Jeffery. "War Consumes South Sudan, a Young Nation Cracking Apart." *The New York Times*, March 4, 2017.

Ghirmazion, Aseghedech. *In Quest for a Culture of Peace in the IGAD Region: The Role of Intellectuals and Scholars*. Nairobi: Heinrich Böll Foundation Regional Office for East Africa and Horn of Africa, 2016.

Gibia, Roba. *John Garang and the Vision of New Sudan*. Toronto: Key Publishing House Inc., 2008.

Gidron, Yotam. "Five Years of War in Blue Nile State: Hope and Despair between the Two Sudans." *Ifriqiya* 2, no. 6 (2016).

Githigaro, John M. "What Went Wrong in South Sudan in December 2013?" *African Conflict & Peacebuilding Review* 6, no. 2 (2016): 112–22.

Healy, Sally. "IGAD and Regional Security in the Horn." In *Routledge Handbook of African Security*, edited by James J. Hentz, 217–28. London: Routledge, 2014.

Healy, Sally. "Peacemaking in the Midst of War: An Assessment of IGAD's Contribution to Regional Security." *Royal Institute of International Affairs*, m, November, 2009.

Hirsh, John L. and Robert Oakley. *Somalia and Operation Restore Hope: Reflections on Peacemaking and Peacekeeping*. Washington, DC: U.S. Institute of Peace, 1995.

Hubbard, Michael, Nicoletta Merlo, Simon Maxwell, and Enzo Caputo. "Regional Food Security Strategies: The Case of IGADD in the Horn of Africa." *Food Policy* 17, no. 1 (1992): 7–22.

Hull, Cecilia and Emma Svensson. *African Union Mission in Somalia (AMISOM): Exemplifying African Union Peacekeeping Challenges.* Stockholm: Swedish Defence Research Agency, 2008.

Human Rights Watch. "Sudan: Events of 2017." https://www.hrw.org/world-report/2018/country-chapters/sudan

"IGAD Suspends South Sudan Peace Revitalization Talks." *Sudan Tribune*, February 17, 2018. http://www.sudantribune.com/spip.php?article64744

Ingiriis, Mohamed H. "Building Peace from the Margins in Somalia: The Case for Political Settlement with Al-Shabaab," *Contemporary Security Policy* February (2018): 1–25.

International Crisis Group. "Ending Starvation as a Weapon of War in Sudan." *Africa Report* No. 54, November 14, 2002.

International Crisis Group. "Salvaging Somalia's Chance for Peace." *Africa Briefing*, December 2002.

International Crisis Group. "Somalia: Countering Terrorism in a Failed State." *Africa Report* No. 45, May 2002.

International Crisis Group, "South Sudan: A Civil War by Any Other Name." *Africa Report* No. 45, May 2002.

International Crisis Group. "South Sudan: Keeping Faith with the IGAD Peace Process." *Africa Report* No. 28, July 27, 2015. https://d2071andvipowj.cloudfront.net/228-south-sudan-keeping-faith-with-the-igad-peace-process.pdf

IRIN. "IGAD to Deploy Peacekeepers Despite Opposition by Faction Leaders." March 16, 2005. http://www.irinnews.org/news/2005/03/15/igad-deploy-peacekeepers-despite-opposition-faction-leaders

IRIN. Stephanie Glinski, "'The Conflict Must End': Fighting Threatens to Drive Up Hunger in South Sudan's Lean Season." July 2, 2018. https://www.irinnews.org/news-feature/2018/07/02/conflict-must-end-fighting-threatens-drive-hunger-south-sudan-s-lean-season

Iyob, Ruth and Gilbert M. Khadiagala. *Sudan: The Elusive Quest for Peace.* Boulder, CO: Lynne Rienner Publishers, 2006.

Johnson, Douglas H. “Briefing: The Crisis in South Sudan.” *African Affairs* 113(451) (2014): 300–9.

Johnson, Douglas H. *South Sudan: A New History for a New Nation.* Athens: Ohio University Press, 2016.

Johnson, Douglas H. “The Political Crisis in South Sudan.” *African Studies Review* 57, no. 3 (2014): 167–74.

Johnson, Douglas H. *The Root Causes of Sudan's Civil Wars.* Bloomington: Indiana University Press, 2013.

Johnson Likoti, Fako. “The 1998 Military Intervention in Lesotho: SADC Peace Mission or Resource War?” *International Peacekeeping* 14, no. 2 (2007): 251–63.

Jok, Jok Madut and Sharon E. Hutchinson. “Sudan's Prolonged Second Civil War and the Militarization of Nuer and Dinka Ethnic Identities.” *African Studies Review* 42, no. 2 (1999): 125–45.

Juma, Monika K. “The Intergovernmental Authority on Development and the East African Community.” In *From Cape to Congo: Southern Africa's Evolving Security Challenges,* edited by Mwesiga Baregu and Christopher Landsberg, 225–55. Boulder, CO: Lynne Rienner Publishers, 2003.

Justice Africa. “Prospects for Peace in Sudan.” Briefing June–July 2004, 5 July 2004. http://www.justiceafrica.org/June_July04.htm

Kaplan, Seth. “The Remarkable Story of Somaliland.” *Journal of Democracy* 19, no. 3 (2008): 143–57.

“Kenya Focus on Peace and Security in the Horn of Africa.” *Diplomacy Bulletin – The Official Bulletin of the Ministry of Foreign Affairs Kenya* 1, no. 2 (2017): 8–9.

Khadiagala, Gilbert M. *Meddlers or Mediators? African Interveners in Civil Conflicts in Eastern Africa.* Leiden: Brill, 2007.

Khadiagala, Gilbert M. “Regional Cooperation on Democratization and Conflict Management in Africa.” *Carnegie Endowment for International Peace,* 2018. http://carnegieendowment.org/2018/03/19/regional-cooperation-on-democratization-and-conflict-management-in-africa-pub-75769

Knopf, Katherine Almquist. “Ending South Sudan's Civil War.” *Council of Foreign Relations, Special Report,* no. 77, November 2016.

Kornprobst, Markus. “The Management of Border Disputes in African Regional Subsystems: Comparing West Africa and the Horn of Africa.” *Journal of Modern African Studies* 40, no. 3 (2002): 369–93.

Kuol, Stephen Par. “South Sudan Crisis: Machar vs. IGAD.” *Sudan Tribune* April 4, 2018. http://www.sudantribune.com/spip.php?article65100

Kwaje, Samson L. "The Sudan Peace Process, From Machakos to Naivasha." In *African Regional Security in the Age of Globalisation*, edited by Makũumi Mwagiru, 96–106. Nairobi: Heinrich Boll Foundation, 2004.

Large, Daniel. "China and South Sudan Civil War, 2013-–2015." *African Studies Quarterly* 16, no. 3–4 (2016): 35–54.

Leach, Justin D. *War and Politics in Sudan: Cultural Identities and the Challenge of the Peace Process.* London: I.B. Tauris, 2013.

Levitt, Jeremy. "Conflict Prevention, Management, and Resolution: Africa – Regional Strategies for the Prevention of Displacement and Protection of Displaced Persons: the Cases of the OAU, ECOWAS, SADC, and IGAD." *Duke Journal of Comparative & International Law* 11 (2000): 39–79.

Lewis, I.M. *Making and Breaking States in Africa: The Somali Experience*. Trenton, NJ: Red Sea Press, 2010.

Maalim, Mahboub. "IGAD's Role in Stability and Diplomacy in the Horn of Africa." *Chatham House Africa Summary*, May 9, 2013. http://www.chathamhouse.org/sites/default/files/public/Research/Africa/090513summary.pdf

Mamdani, Mahmood. "Prof. Mamdani Speech on S. Sudan: Part II." *New Vision* February 18, 2014. https://www.newvision.co.ug/new_vision/news/1337818/prof-mamdani-speech-sudan-ii

Maru, Mehari T. "IGAD-Migration Action Plan (MAP) to operationalize The IGAD Regional Migration Policy Framework (IGAD-RMPF) 2015–2020." http://migration.igad.int/wp-content/uploads/2017/02/IGAD-Migration-Action-Plan-MAP-2015-2020.pdf

Maru, Mehari T. "Migration Priorities and Normative and Institutional Framework in the IGAD Region." *Horn of Africa Bulletin* August 28, 2015. http://life-peace.org/hab/migration-priorities-and-normative-and-institutional-frameworks-in-the-igad-region/

Mason, Simon A. "Learning from the Swiss Mediation and Facilitation Experiences in Sudan." *Working paper, Mediation Support Project.* Zurich: Center for Security Studies, ETH Zurich & swisspeace, 2007. http://www.isn.ethz.ch/news/dossier/mediation/pubs/pub.cfm

McHugh, Neil. *Holy Men of the Blue Nile: the Making of an Arab-Islamic Community in the Nilotic Sudan, 1500–1850*. Evanston, IL: Northwestern University Press, 1994.

Medani, Khalid Mustafa. "Strife and Secession in Sudan." *Journal of Democracy* 22, no. 3 (2011): 135–49.

Menkhaus, Kenneth J. "Governance without Government in Somalia: Spoilers, State Building, and the Politics of Coping." *International Security* 31, no. 3 (2006/07): 74–106.

Menkhaus, Kenneth J. "State Collapse in Somalia: Second Thoughts." *Review of African Political Economy* 30 (2003): 405–22.

Menkhaus, Ken J., Hassan Sheikh, Ali Joqombe, and Pat Johnson. "The Search for Peace, Somali Programme: A History of Mediation in Somalia since 1988." *Interpeace: International Peace Alliance,* May 2009.

Miti, Katabaro, "South Africa and Conflict Resolution in Africa: From Mandela to Zuma." *Southern African Peace and Security Studies* 1, no. 1 (2012): 27–30.

Moritz, Lodiyong. "South Sudan, Uganda in Border Dilemma." *The Niles Editors* August 7, 2011.

Mulama, Joyce. "Darfur Overshadows the Peace Process in South Sudan." *Sudan Tribune,* September 2, 2004. http://www.sudantribune.com/spip.php?article5175

Mulugeta, Kidist. "The Role of Regional and International Organizations in Resolving the Somali Conflict: The Case of IGAD." *Friedrich Ebert-Stiftung,* Addis Ababa, December 2010.

Murithi, Tim. "Inter-governmental Authority on Development on the Ground: Comparing Interventions in Sudan and Somalia." *African Security* 2, no. 2–3 (2009): 137–57.

Nairobi Forum. "IGAD and Somalia." October 25, 2013. file:///C:/Users/a/Downloads/RVI%20-%20Nairobi%20Forum%20-%20Meeting%20Report%20-%20IGAD%20and%20Somalia%20(1).pdf

Natsios, Andrew S. *Sudan, South Sudan, and Darfur: What Everyone Needs to Know.* New York: Oxford University Press, 2012.

Nzongola-Ntalaja, Georges. "Civil War, Peacekeeping and the Great Lakes region." In *The Causes of War and Consequences of Peacekeeping in Africa,* edited by Ricardo R. Laremont, 116–26. Portsmouth, NH: Heinemann, 2002.

Obonyo, Raphael. "Peace in South Sudan Critical to Regional Stability." *Africa Renewal,* August 2014. https://www.un.org/africarenewal/magazine/august-2014/peace-south-sudan-critical-regional-stability

Oluoch, Fred. "What Prospects for a Lasting Peace in South Sudan?" *New African,* (2016): 16–17. http://newafricanmagazine.com/prospects-lasting-peace-south-sudan/

Patey, Luke A. "Crude Days Ahead? Oil and the Resource Curse in Sudan." *African Affairs* 109 (2010): 617–36.

Peskin, Victor. "Caution and Confrontation in the International Criminal Court's Pursuit of Accountability in Uganda and Sudan." *Human Rights Quarterly* 31 (2009): 655–91.

Pham, Peter J. "State Collapse, Insurgency, and Famine in the Horn of Africa: Legitimacy and the Ongoing Somali Crisis." *The Middle East Journal of the Middle East and Africa* 2, no. 2 (2011): 153–87.

Poggo, Scopas A. *The First Sudanese Civil War: Africans, Arabs, and Israelis in the Southern Sudan, 1955–1972.* New York: Palgrave Macmillan, 2009.

"Powell Declares Genocide in Sudan." *BBC News,* September 9, 2004. http://news.bbc.co.uk/2/hi/3641820.stm

"President Ahmed Mohamed Silanyo Strongly Condemned a Communiqué Released by IGAD Leaders in Mogadishu." September 17, 2016. http://somalilandrise.com/articles/5096/President-Ahmed-Mohamed-Silanyo-strongly-condemned-a-communique-released-by-IGAD-leaders-in-Mogadishu

Prunier, Gérard. *Africa's World War: Congo, the Rwanda Genocide, and the Making of a Continental Catastrophe*. New York: Oxford University Press, 2009.

Prunier, Gérard. *Darfur: The Ambiguous Genocide*, Ithaca, NY: Cornell University Press, 2005.

Prunier, Gérard. "Somalia: Civil War, Intervention and Withdrawal." *Refugee Survey Quarterly* 15, no. 1 (1996): 35–85.

Quartz Africa. "These Nine Charts Tell You What's in Store for Africa in 2018." January 3, 2018. https://qz.com/1168720/africa-in-2018-ticking-debt-bomb-internet-shutdowns-startups-innovation-and-visa-travels/

Reeve, Richard. "Peace and Conflict Assessment of South Sudan." *International Alert Organization*, 2012. http://www.international-alert.org/sites/default/files/SouthSudan_PeaceConflictAssessment_EN_2012.pdf

Reliefweb. "South Sudanese Parties Sign Agreements on Cessation of Hostilities and Question of Detainees." January 23, 2014. https://reliefweb.int/report/south-sudan-republic/south-sudanese-parties-sign-agreements-cessation-hostilities-and

Reno, William. "The Regionalization of African Security." *Current History* 111, no. 745 (2011): 175–80.

Republic of Uganda. Press Briefing by Hon. Sam K. Kutesa, Minister of Foreign Affairs, regarding South Sudan, February 18, 2014. https://www.mofa.go.ug/data/dnews/21/PRESS%20BRIEFING%20BY%20HON.%20SAM%20K.%20KUTESA,%20MINISTER%20OF%20FOREIGN%20AFFAIRS,%20REGARDING%20SOUTH%20SUDAN.html

Roach, Steven A. "South Sudan: A Volatile Dynamic of Accountability and Peace." *International Affairs* 92, no. 6 (2016): 1343–59.

Rolandsen, Øystein H. "Another Civil War in South Sudan: the Failure of Guerrilla Government?" *Journal of Eastern African Studies* 9, no. 1 (2015): 163–74.

Rolandsen, Øystein H. and M.W. Daly. *A History of South Sudan: From Slavery to Independence*. Cambridge: Cambridge University Press, 2016.

Rupesinghe, Kumar. *Conflict Transformation*. London: Macmillan, 1995.

Sandu, Ciprian. "The South Sudan Coup: A Political Rivalry that Turned Ethnic." *Conflict Studies Quarterly* 7 (2014): 49–65.

Sengupta, Somini. "In South Sudan, Some Lessons of Rwanda Learned, Others Revisited." *New York Times*, January 16, 2014. https://www.nytimes.com/2014/01/17/world/africa/in-south-sudan-some-lessons-of-rwanda-learned-others-revisited.html

Shillinger, Kurt. *Africa's Peace Maker? Lessons from South African Conflict Mediation*. Auckland Park: Jacana, 2009.

Shinn, David H. "Addis Ababa Agreement: Was it Destined to Fail and are there Lessons for the Current Sudan Peace Process?" *Annales d'Ethiopie* 20 (2004): 239–59.

Siebert John, "R2P and the IGAD Sub-region: IGAD's Contribution to Africa's Emerging R2P-oriented Security Culture." In *Crafting an African Security Architecture: Addressing Regional Peace and Conflict in the 21th Century*, edited by Hany Besada, 89–108. Routledge, 2010.

Smillie, Ian and Larry Minear. *The Charity of Nations: Humanitarian Action in a Calculating World*. Bloomfield: Kumarian Press, 2004.

Soliman, Ahmed and Aly Verjee. "How to Support South Sudan's High Level Revitalization Forum." *Chatham House* 29, 2017. https://www.chathamhouse.org/expert/comment/how-support-south-sudan-s-high-level-revitalization-forum

"South Sudan-IGAD Warning." *Africa Research Bulletin* 51, no. 7 (2014): 29490–1.

South Sudan News Agency (SSNA). "Exclusive: IGAD-led Peace Talks are not Convincing." November 15, 2014. http://southsudannewsagency.org/index.php/2014/11/16/exclusive-igad-led-peace-talks-are-not-convincing/

Spittaels, Steven and Yannick Weyns. "Mapping Conflict Motives: the Sudan – South Sudan border." *International Peace Information Service (IPIS) Report*, January 2014.

Stein, Janice G. "From Bipolar to Unipolar Order: System Structure and Conflict Resolution." In *International Intervention in Local Conflicts: Crisis Management and Conflict Resolution since the Cold War*, edited by Uzi Rabi, 3–18. London: I.B. Tauris, 2010.

Stringham, Noel and Jonathan Forney. "It Takes a Village to Raise a Militia: Local Politics, the Nuer White Army, and South Sudan's Civil Wars." *Journal of Modern African Studies* 55, no. 2 (2017): 177–99.

"Sudan: Abyei Seizure by North 'Act of War', Says South." *BBC News*, May 22, 2011.

Sudan Tribune. "IGAD appoints former Botswana president to head monitoring commission on South Sudan." October 20, 2015. http://www.sudantribune.com/spip.php?article56773

Sudan Tribune. "Kenya Invites Bashir to IGAD Summit as he Challenges World to Arrest Him." March 4, 2010. http://www.sudantribune.com/spip.php?article34312

Sudan Tribune. "S. Sudan Launches Conflict Early Warning and Response Unit." May 9, 2012. http://www.sudantribune.com/spip.php?article42544

Sudan Tribune. "South Sudan President Delays 2015 General Elections." May 13, 2014. http://www.sudantribune.com/spip.php?article50982

Sudan Tribune. "South Sudan President Will Not Discuss Abyei in Khartoum." October 28, 2017. http://www.sudantribune.com/spip.php?article63864

Sudan Tribune. "IGAD Suspends South Sudan Revitalization Talks." February 16, 2018. http://www.sudantribune.com/spip.php?article64744

Sudan Tribune. "Sudan, IGAD Discuss Resumption of Two Areas Peace Talks." September 28, 2017. http://www.sudantribune.com/spip.php?article63617

Sudd Institute. "South Sudan's Crisis: Its Drivers, Key Players, and Post-conflict Prospects." *Special Report* August 3, 2014. https://www.suddinstitute.org/assets/Publications/572b7eb3cea73_SouthSudansCrisisItsDriversKeyPlayers_Full.pdf

Tanza, John. "South Sudan Warring Parties Ink a Cease-Fire Deal." *VOA News*, December 22, 2017. https://www.voanews.com/a/negotiations-to-end-four-year-conflict-in-south-sudan/4174880.html

Tavares, Rodrigo. "The Participation of SADC and ECOWAS in Military Operations: The Weight of National Interests in Decision-Making." *African Studies Review* 54, no. 2 (2011): 145–76.

Tekle, Amere. "The Basis of Eritrean-Ethiopian Cooperation." In *Eritrea and Ethiopia: From Conflict to Cooperation*, edited by Amare Tekle, 1–20. Lawrenceville, NJ: Red Sea Press, 1994.

The Guardian. "Somalia Famine in 2010–12 Worst in Past 25 Years." May 2, 2013. https://www.theguardian.com/global-development/2013/may/02/somalia-famine-worst-25-years

Uma, Julius N. "S. Sudan Launches Conflict Early Warning and Response Unit." *Sudan Tribune*, May 9, 2012.

Vines, Alex. "A Decade of African Peace and Security Architecture." *International Affairs* 89, no. 1 (2013): 89–109.

Waihenya, Waithaka. *The Mediator. Gen. Lazaro Sumbeiywo and the Southern Sudan Peace Process*. Nairobi: Kenway Publications, 2006.

Weiss, Thomas G. *Humanitarian Intervention: Ideas in Action*. Cambridge: Polity Press, 2009.

Weldesellassie, K. Isaac. "IGAD as an International Organization, Its Institutional Development and Shortcomings." *Journal of African Law* 55, no. 1 (2011): 1–29.

Wight, Patrick. "South Sudan and the Four Dimensions of Power-Sharing: Political, Territorial, Military, and Economic." *African Conflict & Peacebuilding Review* 7, no. 2 (2017): 1–35.

Wild, Hannah, Jok M. Jok, and Ronak Pate. "The Militarization of Cattle Raiding in South Sudan: How a Traditional Practice Became a Tool for Political Violence." *International Journal of Humanitarian Action* 3, no. 2 (2018): 1–11.

Wöndu, Steven and Ann Lesch. *Battle for Peace in Sudan: An Analysis of the Abuja Conferences 1992–93*. Lanham, MD: University Press of America, 2000.

Woodward, Peter. "Somalia and Sudan: A Tale of Two Peace Processes." *The Round Table* 93, no. 375 (2004): 469–81.

Yabi, Gilles. "Keeping the Peace in Electoral Conflicts: The Role of ECOWAS, UNOCI and the International Community in Côte d'Ivoire." *ZIF: Center for International Peace Operations*, October 2012. http://www.zif-berlin.org/fileadmin/uploads/analyse/dokumente/veroeffentlichungen/ZIF_Policy_Briefing_Gilles_Yabi_Oct_2012.pdf

Yihun, Belete B. "Ethiopia's Role in South Sudan's March to Independence, 1955–1991." *African Studies Quarterly* 14, no. 1 & 2 (2013): 35–54.

Ylönen, Aleksi. "Security Regionalism and Flaws of Externally Forged Peace in Sudan: The IGAD Peace Process and its Aftermath." *African Journal of Conflict Resolution* 14, no. 2 (2014): 13–39.

Ylönen, Aleksi. "The Sudan-South Sudan Military Escalation in Heglig: Shifting Attention from Domestic Challenges." *Conflict Trends* 4 (2012): 11–19.

Young, John. "John Garang's Legacy to the Peace Process, the SPLM/A & the south." *Review of African Political Economy* 32, no. 106 (2005): 535–48.

Young, John. "Sudan IGAD Peace Process; An Evaluation." *Sudan Tribune*, May 30, 2007. https://www.sudantribune.com/IMG/pdf/Igad_in_Sudan_Peace_Process.pdf

Young, John. "The South Sudan Defence Forces in the Wake of the Juba Declaration." http://www.smallarmssurveysudan.org/fileadmin/docs/working-papers/HSBA-WP-01-SSDF.pdf

Young, John. "SPLM-NORTH: What Went Wrong?" *Sudan Tribune*, April 3, 2018. http://www.sudantribune.com/spip.php?article65091

Zartman, William I. *Ripe for Resolution: Conflict and Intervention in Africa*. New York: Oxford University Press, 1985.

Zartman, William I. "Ripeness: The Hurting Stalemate and Beyond." In *International Conflict Resolution after the Cold War*, edited by Paul Stern and Daniel Druckman, 225–50. Washington, DC: National Academy Press, 2000.

Zweifel, Thomas D. *International Organizations and Democracy: Accountability, Politics, and Power*. Boulder, CO: Lynne Rienner, 2006.

African Union (by Date)

Constitutive Act of the African Union, Article 4(h), July 11, 2000. http://www.au.int/en/sites/default/files/ConstitutiveAct_EN.pdf

Comprehensive Peace Agreement between the Government of the Republic of Sudan and the Sudan People Liberation Movement/Army. https://peacemaker.un.org/sites/peacemaker.un.org/files/SD_060000_The%20Comprehensive%20Peace%20Agreement.pdf

Report on the Status of the Establishment of the Continental Peace and Security Architecture, Presented at the 57th meeting of the PSC, June 21, 2006, Addis Ababa, Ethiopia. Reference: PSC/PR/(LVII).

AU Peace and Security Council (Somalia) Communiqué, PSC/PR/Comm. (LXIX), January 19, 2007.

Final Report of the African Union Commission of Inquiry on South Sudan – Executive Summary, Addis-Ababa, October 15, 2014. https://reliefweb.int/sites/reliefweb.int/files/resources/auciss.executive.summary.pdf

European Union (EU)

"Factsheet: The EU and South Sudan." July 10, 2014. https://reliefweb.int/report/south-sudan/factsheet-eu-and-south-sudan10-july-2014

"Joint Press Release by the EU and IGAD on the Informal Ministerial Meeting with Foreign Ministers from IGAD Member Countries." Bruxelles, September 29, 2017. https://eeas.europa.eu/headquarters/headquarters-homepage/33065/joint-press-release-eu-and-igad-informal-ministerial-meeting-foreign-ministers-igad-member_en

IGADD

"The Inter-Governmental Authority on Drought and Development (IGADD)." *Review of African Political Economy* 21, no. 59 (1994): 93–5.

IGAD *(by Date)*

The IGAD Declaration of Principles, Nairobi, May 20, 1994. https://peacemaker.un.org/sudan-igad-principles94

Agreement Establishing the Inter-Governmental Authority on Development (IGAD), Nairobi, March 21, 1996. IGAD/SUM-96/AGRE-Doc, http://peacemaker.un.org/sites/peacemaker.un.org/files/SD_940520_The%20IGAD% "Koka Dam Declaration." http://peacemaker.un.org/sudan-kokadam-declaration86

Proceedings of the Eighth Ordinary IGAD Summit of Heads of States and Government, November 23, 2000, Khartoum, Republic of Sudan.

Khartoum Declaration of the Eighth Summit of Heads of State and Government, Khartoum, November 23, 2000 (A/55/726-S/2001/3). http://reliefweb.int/report/djibouti/khartoum-declaration-eighth-summit-heads-state-and-government-khartoum-23-nov-2000

Agreed text on the Right for Self-Determination for the People of South Sudan. The Machakos Protocol (or Chapter I), signed in Machakos, Kenya, July 20, 2002.

Report on IGAD Conference on the Prevention and Combating of Terrorism UN Conference Centre, Addis Ababa, June 24–27, 2003.

"The Mediator's Perspective: An interview with General Lazaro Sumbeiywo." http://www.c-r.org/downloads/Accord%2018_8The%20mediator's%20perspective_2006_ENG.pdf

"Statement by the Executive Secretary of IGAD Ambassador Mahboub M. Maalim on the Successful Neutralization of al-Shabab Terrorist Attack at the Westgate Mall and the Regional Way Forward." October 24, 2013. https://igad.int/attachments/676_Statement_by_IGAD_ES_Complete.pdf

"The Executive Secretary of IGAD AMB. (ENG) Mahboub M. Maalim, Condemns the Unilateral 'Referendum' in Abyei." *IGAD Press Release,* November 3, 2013. https://igad.int/attachments/697_APRESSRELEASEABYEI_opt.pdf

Agreement on the Status of Detainees between the Government of the Republic of South Sudan (GRSS) and the Sudan People's Liberation Movement/Army (In-Opposition) SPLM/A (In-Opposition), January 23, 2014. https://reliefweb.int/report/south-sudan-republic/south-sudanese-parties-sign-agreements-cessation-hostilities-and

Resolutions by the 28th Extraordinary Summit of the IGAD Heads of State and Government, Addis Ababa, November 7, 2014. https://igad.int/index.php?option=com_content&view=article&id=993:resolutions-from-the-28th-extra-ordinary-summit-of-heads-of-state-and-government&catid=61:statements

9th Annual Joint Consultative Meeting between African Union Peace and Security Council (AUPSC) and the United Nation Security Council (UNSC), Addis Ababa, March 12, 2015. http://www.peaceau.org/en/article/joint-communique-of-the-9th-annual-joint-consultative-meeting-between-african-union-peace-and-security-council-aupsc-and-the-united-nations-security-council-unsc-addis-ababa-12-march-2015

Opening Statement by the Chairperson of the IGAD Special Envoys for South Sudan; "LATEST: IGAD Special Envoys Congratulate South Sudan on Peace Signing" https://igad.int/index.php?option=com_content&view=article&id=1197:igad-special-envoys-congratulate-south-sudan-on-peace-signing&catid=1:latest-news&Itemid=150

"Agreement on the Resolution of the Conflict in the Republic of South Sudan." Addis Ababa, Ethiopia, August 17, 2015. https://unmiss.unmissions.org/sites/default/files/final_proposed_compromise_agreement_for_south_sudan_conflict.pdf

Opening Statement by the Chairperson of the IGAD Special Envoys for South Sudan. August 6, 2015, Addis Ababa. https://southsudan.igad.int/attachments/article/298/080715_EnvoysOpenningStatement.pdf

"JMEC Agreement Summary." http://jmecsouthsudan.org/index.php/arcss-2015

"Communiqué of the Second IGAD PLUS Extraordinary Summit on the Situation in the Republic of South Sudan." August 5, 2016. https://igad.int/attachments/article/1383/1408_AGREED%20FINAL%20COMMUNIQUE%20-%20IGAD%20Plus%20on%20South%20Sudan%20in%20Addis.pdf

Communiqué of 28th IGAD Extraordinary Summit on Somalia, September 13, 2016. https://igad.int/communique/1351-communique-of-the-28th-igad-extra-ordinary-summit-on-somalia

"Briefing to the IGAD Extraordinary Summit on the Situation in South Sudan by United Nations Special Representative of the Secretary-General David Shearer." June 12, 2017. https://unmiss.unmissions.org/sites/default/files/statement_of_srsg_shearer_to_the_igad.pdf

High level Revitalization Forum for the Resolution of the Conflict in South Sudan Concluded with Signing of an Agreement on Cessation of Hostilities. December 18, 2017.

https://igad.int/programs/115-south-sudan-office/1731-high-level-revitalization-forum-agreement-on-cessation-of-hostilities-protection-of-civilians-and-humanitarian-access-republic-of-south-sudan

Nairobi Declaration on Durable Solutions for Somali Refugees and Reintegration of Returnees in Somalia. March 25, 2017. https://igad.int/communique/1519-communique-special-summit-of-the-igad-assembly-of-heads-of-state-and-government-on-durable-solutions-for-somali-refugees

Communiqué of the 32nd Extra-Ordinary Summit of IGAD Assembly of Heads of State and Government on South Sudan. June 21, 2018. https://igad.int/attachments/article/1865/Final%20Communique%20of%20the%2032nd%20IGAD%20Summit.pdf

SADC (*by Date*)

"Protocol on Politics, Defense and Security in Southern Africa Development Community (SADC) region." Maseru, Lesotho, June 30, 1996.

SADC *Regional Human Development Report 2000: Challenges and Opportunities for Regional Integration.* Harare, Zimbabwe: SAPES Books, 2000.

Global and Inclusive Agreement on Transition in the Democratic Republic of the Congo. Signed in Pretoria, Republic of South Africa, December 16, 2002. http://peacemaker.un.org/sites/peacemaker.un.org/files/CD_021216_Global%20and%20Inclusive%20Agreement%20on%20Transition%20in%20DRC.pdf

UN (by Date)

United Nations Security Council, "Report of the Secretary-General on Liberia." Security Council Documents s/26422. September 9, 1993.

Final Report of the Secretary-General on the UN Observer Mission in Liberia, S/1997/712/12. September 1997.

"The Regional Economic Communities (RECs) of the African Union." http://www.un.org/en/africa/osaa/peace/recs.shtml

"Full, Timely Implementation of Sudan's Comprehensive Peace Agreement Essential to National, Regional Stability, Security Council Presidential Statement Says." 6425th Meeting, November 16, 2010. https://www.un.org/press/en/2010/sc10086.doc.htm

United Nation Mission in South Sudan (UNMISS). Interim Report on Human Rights: Crisis in South Sudan; Report Coverage. December 15, 2013–January 31, 2014.

"Uprooted by Conflict: South Sudan's Displacement Crisis." *International Rescue Committee*, November 2014; Report of the Secretary-General on South Sudan (covering the period from April 14 to August 19, 2015). http://www.un.org/en/ga/search/view_doc.asp?symbol=S/2015/655

"Ban Welcomes New Agreement with Inter Parliamentary Union; Reiterates Concern at South Sudan Crisis." *UN News*, July 21, 2016. https://news.un.org/en/story/

2016/07/535102-ban-welcomes-new-agreement-inter-parliamentary-union-reiterates-concern-south
OCHA. *South Sudan Humanitarian Bulletin*, Issue 14. September 8, 2017. https://reliefweb.int/report/south-sudan/south-sudan-humanitarian-bulletin-issue-14-08-september-2017

Personal Interviews

Interview with IGAD official, IGAD, Addis Ababa, August 10, 2017.
Interview with Mearuf Nurhusein, IGAD, Addis Ababa, August 10, 2017.
Interview with Dr. Sunday Okello, African Union Peace and Security Programme, Addis Ababa University, August 14, 2017.
Interview with Ambassador Ismail Wais, Special IGAD Envoy to South Sudan, Addis Ababa, May 3, 2018.
Interview with Kenyan Diplomat, Kenya Embassy in Israel, Ramat Gan, February 15, 2018.
Interview with Dr. Yonas Adaye, African Union Peace and Security Programme, Addis Ababa University, May 5, 2018.

Index

Printed in the United States
By Bookmasters